Finding I[ntimacy] with Jesus Made Simple

Key Truths to Draw You Closer

Matthew Robert Payne

Finding Intimacy with Jesus Made Simple

More information about Matthew can be found at
http://www.matthewrobertpayneministries.net

Matthew also can be found on Facebook in a group that he runs called "Open Heavens and Intimacy with Jesus." that can be found here
https://www.facebook.com/groups/OpenHeavensGroup/

Matthew has written several other books before this one and they can be found on his Amazon author page here:

http://www.amazon.com/Matthew-Robert-Payne/e/B008N9R896/ref=ntt_athr_dp_pel_1

Editor: Melanie Cardano from www.upwork.com

The opinions expressed by the author are not necessarily those of Revival Waves of Glory Books & Publishing.

Revival Waves of Glory Books & Publishing
PO Box 596
Litchfield, IL 62056
United States of America
www.revivalwavesofgloryministries.com

Revival Waves of Glory Books & Publishing is committed to excellence in the publishing industry.

Published in the United States of America

Paperback: 978-1-365-76011-2

Hardcover: 978-1-365-90412-7

Table of Contents

Dedication

Bob Payne

You took me into your family and raised me the best way that you knew how. Though we had some rocky days, your love for me and our relationship has blossomed and I pray that you will enjoy this 13th book of your son.

To the Hungry Hearts.

If you are hungry after the presence of Jesus and to be able to walk in the Spirit then this book is for you. If you want Jesus to be closer to you, I pray that my simple words in this book will take you to another level.

Acknowledgements:

Jesus

I want to thank You, Jesus, for being my lifelong friend. You have been with me through all the sins, through all the bad times, and You are still with me as my life seems to be going really well. I am happy to produce another book that You had planned for me to write before I was born. All praise and honor goes to you.

Father

I want to thank You for giving me Your Son and the Holy Spirit. This book was written when I didn't know you so well. I'm thankful that You have brought healing in my life and that now, we are getting to know each other. Like a father and son playing soccer we are enjoying each other.

Holy Spirit

Thank You for leading me, guiding me, fashioning me and co-writing this book with me.

June Payne

Thank you for pre-editing this book and being my other, who believes in me. You know how special you are.

Bryn Phillips

Thank you for your generous donation to my ministry, so that this book could be published.

Melanie Cardano

I want to thank you for your copy editing and proofreading and your love and support of all my work. I want to thank you also for your creative writing to make the back cover of this book. Melanie can be hired as a Freelance worker from www.Upwork.com.

Bill Vincent of Revival Waves of Glory Ministries - Books & Publishing

Thank you for your belief in me, your time and your professionalism in publishing my book and getting it into the marketplace.

Introduction

One day, the Holy Spirit told me to take a notepad of paper and a pen into my community center where I serve coffee three days a week. I took the pen and notepad. I was due to meet a young girl and we were going to go and visit a church I was attending at the time. While I was waiting for her, the Holy Spirit gave me a number of subjects to write on. He told me it was going to be a new book and He gave me the subjects I was going to write about one by one. When I had about sixteen subjects, He had me start to write headings under each of the sixteen subjects. I wrote about eight to ten headings under each subject.

The book you hold in your hand is what the Holy Spirit led me to say about each of the subjects. It is my prayer that each truth may go past your mind and down into your spirit. I hope that this book might not only be read once, but you might use this book again as a devotional, ponder deeply and reflect on each truth These truths are simple ones about the Kingdom of God that I have come to know and understand. I pray that this book will bring you into a greater dimension of intimacy.

I have not arrived, and I could be wrong in some of what I say, and yet, in my humble observation as I read this today, two years after originally writing it, I cannot see any error. I pray that you will be blessed reading it just as I was blessed to write and prepare it for you to read.

This book has a history. Originally published with a title that wasn't very descriptive, and a cover that wasn't really professional, it had luck lustre sales. I have now re- titled it and given it a more professional cover and the result is what you are reading now. I refer to each truth presented as a Kingdom Nugget as the original book was called Kingdom Nuggets.

Matthew Robert Payne

January 2016

Kingdom Nugget 1
Leaving Heaven for Earth

Jesus willingly left Heaven's perfect environment, where there is no sickness, disease or death. Neither are there such things as threats, violence, accidents or any type of pain in Heaven. Therefore, every type of heartache, including inadequacy, fear, loneliness or rejection doesn't exist! Sin and its consequences have no part in God's glorious Heaven.

To fulfil His Father's mission, Jesus came to a place full of disease but with no healers, a place where babies were harmed when He was born and where His adult life was under threat. He came to a place of imperfection called earth.

Sin reigned everywhere on Earth. This new home for the precious Son of God was filled with heartache, self-centeredness, greed, violence, sickness, decay, pride, prejudice, rebellion, injustice and death. The life of Jesus on earth was totally opposite to His life in Heaven.

To the spirit of Jesus and the Holy Spirit within Him, the earth was a terrible place. Jesus willingly left Heaven knowing that His life on earth was going to be a trial. He came from perfection to that which was corrupt. We need to understand this about Jesus before anything else. He was no ordinary human from birth to ascension. He was the Son of God who came down from Heaven.

Kingdom Nugget 2
A Hard Life On Earth

Growing up, Jesus was ridiculed and laughed at by James, his younger brother. He was constantly teased by His siblings for being mom and dad's favorite! He lived with the revelation that His entire life would be difficult and at His Heavenly Father's appointed time, He would die a cruel and public death. Yet, for just one festive day, He was publicly and briefly hailed by a cheering and enthusiastic crowd - as the long-awaited Messiah King.

Jesus was never fully understood. Emotionally, He carried His cross from His birth to the grave. It can be hard for us to fully comprehend but Jesus was out of this world. Many of us have been teased and ridiculed and so we can relate to that. But Jesus never retaliated to any of the teasing or mocking. Jesus had the whole of Hell going out of its way, coming against Him, trying to make Him sin. Long before Jesus was tempted in the wilderness, He was tempted on earth.

Jesus lived a hard life on earth so that through his death and blood, we can have peace and a more joyful life of overcoming. Jesus suffered so we don't need to suffer as much. Some people assume that the only hard thing Jesus went though was the cross and this is wrong. Jesus' whole life was hard.

Kingdom Nugget 3
A Life of Mocking

Have you ever had siblings who disliked your pure spirit? Jesus was mocked by His brothers because He was pure in heart and innocent.

Outsiders may have labelled Him a bastard because He was conceived out of wedlock! That was a shameful thing in those days. There was shame hanging over his family.

When Jesus started His public ministry and people started to follow Him as a modern answer to society, there arose another group of mockers who had terrible things to say about Him to others and to His face. To the learned and educated in the things of God, Jesus was rejected and mocked. The Pharisees detested Jesus and went out of their way to mock Him publicly.

The Pharisees' opinion of Jesus led many people astray as they were the experts in all things of the Law. Seeing people influenced by them made Jesus suffer even more.

Then, after a life of misunderstanding and mocking, Jesus went to the cross and the volume of the mocking was raised as the people yelled "Crucify Him!"

And whilst on that cross, Jesus asked His Father to "forgive them for they know not what they do."

Kingdom Nugget 4
Rejection

In the eyes of others, it would have seemed that Jesus was an unplanned child. This was because Mary and Joseph were engaged but not actually married when Jesus was conceived. In fact, Joseph had already planned to quietly break off the relationship. However, God organized a divine angelic intervention to occur, which subsequently caused Joseph to change his mind.

Although Joseph was publicly recognized as the father of Jesus, he and Mary both knew he wasn't the real father. Mary and Joseph knew that this firstborn Son had been miraculously conceived by the Holy Spirit and not by man. Therefore, because of His godly character, Jesus would have been considered very different from other boys his age.

Coming from a highly respected and devout Jewish family, Jesus would have been encouraged to memorize most of the Torah, and to know the books on the prophets by the time He was twelve, for this was a Jewish custom that was vigorously followed. Although Jesus could probably have been a teacher, Jewish law stated that a Rabbi was not recognized as such until he was thirty years old. So He had to wait eighteen years to become a Rabbi.

In that time, he was probably mocked by his siblings and taunted by some people as being a little too smart for his years.

When Jesus began His ministry, rejection by both the authorities and the religious leaders had set in. The Jewish leaders used to conduct tests and studies on any Jew who claimed to be the long awaited Messiah. As time went on, these leaders would have seen that Jesus passed every Messianic proof and still, they totally rejected Him as their long awaited Messiah.

After a three year ministry, Jesus, at thirty-three years old, was publically crucified like a common criminal – the charge: a traitor to Rome! He had been rejected by the very people He had come to save. Have you been rejected? You can be very sure that Jesus knows and understands your personal pain.

Kingdom Nugget 5
The Secret Truths

Have you ever had knowledge about a person, or situation that only you seem privy to? Have you ever had God show you something in His Word, or through a prophetic word, or through a vision or a dream, or maybe through a two way chat with God that absolutely flies in the face of conventional knowledge?

Solomon said: *"For in much wisdom is much grief, and he who increases knowledge increases sorrow." Ecclesiastes 1:18*

Do you realize that when Jesus was only a boy, He would have read in the Book of Psalms that one day, His Own back was going to be ripped to shreds? His back would be stripped as a plough strips through soil, ready for planting. *"The plowers plowed on my back. They made their furrows long." Psalm 129:3*

One day, as I sat in church, Jesus personally and briefly appeared to me. That day, I saw His whipped and beaten body just as if He was about to be hung on the Cross. When He turned His back, I could see it was full of gaping parallel holes. I'm certain that His back, even with today's medical technology, would be permanently and horribly disfigured.

As a serious student of the Prophets, Jesus would have known that what the leaders and teachers of His day were teaching about the Messiah was not right, because their teaching had one major error. The Scribes and Pharisees, as well as the spiritual leaders, could only see in Scripture a conquering King who would one day save Israel from the oppression of Roman rule. Therefore, they eagerly awaited the arrival of this mighty conquering Messiah. This was their constant hope as they interpreted the Old Testament Prophets and Psalms.

However, Jesus, full of the Holy Spirit, rightly saw two comings of the Messiah – First: God's suffering Servant's horrific death and glorious resurrection, and much later: God's Jewish Messiah returning as King of Kings to set up His earthly Kingdom in Jerusalem.

Jesus tried repeatedly to share the truth of Scripture with His disciples, but at that stage, they could not spiritually understand what He was talking about. They were simple fishermen who left religious studies to those who were better equipped to teach it.

There is much sorrow and loneliness in profound revelation. But it's the price you have to pay to be a real friend of God and to share in His secrets. Do you want to choose that kind of life for yourself?

Walking With the Holy Spirit

Have you ever been in a place where you are not in control? It can be a very scary place to be because it can be like crossing a raging river and it's getting too deep for you to stand up in. The current seems to be too strong for it to be safe to continue any further. Caught in that position, you will wonder whether you will keep pressing forward despite the escalating fear inside you! In situations like this, the tough people are sorted out from the weak.

Jesus had only just been water baptized when He was led by the Holy Spirit to face Satan's temptation in the wilderness. His humanity was severely tested three times, before Satan departed. He had not eaten for forty long days and He was in a totally weakened state;   mentally and physically. But in His spirit, He was rejoicing, for He had successfully overcome Satan's three temptations by quoting the Word of God to His enemy.

His wilderness experience certainly would have been far more terrifying than facing a raging current in a mighty river. Fear could have stopped Him in His tracks, but because of the power of the indwelling Holy Spirit, He knew that Satan could not win because His mission had to be completed.

One of His first public appearances was quite a spectacle because He went into the Jewish Temple and in a flying rage, drove out the traders and money changers with a whip! These people had been buying and selling merchandise in His Father's House of prayer.

What sort of early public witness would that be to a ministry that was to magnify God's wisdom, love and power? What kind of reaction would you receive today if you went into a huge popular church and went crazy whipping people who were selling Christian books or buying their Mp3s?

Jesus did everything the Holy Spirit led Him to do and say. He brought Lazarus back from the dead, even with the knowledge that this act of compassion was going to be signing His own death warrant.

Today, we are to bear in mind that the Holy Spirit always knows what's best for us, in order to bring God's glory in our life. But not all He tells us to do will be easy for us to obey.

Reliance On His Father

If the Bible was our only source of revelation, then the early years of Jesus would remain a total mystery to us. In the time of Jesus, only the Old Testament had been written. Because of an insatiable need for pastors and teachers to back up everything they say with a Scripture or two, people are very wary of others who bring forth information that has only been revealed through visions or by a direct conversation with God.

For example: At what age did Jesus know that His real Father was in Heaven? This particular information is not openly revealed to us in the Bible. However, it's recorded that on at least one occasion, Jesus chose to seek His Heavenly Father's business, rather than that of His parents. When He was twelve years old, a very important year for a young Jewish lad, rather than travel and stay put with His parents, Jesus went to have a chat with the learned religious teachers and scribes in the Temple.

Jesus knew a lot even at that young age because it's recorded in Scripture that these leaders in the Temple were astonished at His superior knowledge and the authority in His teaching. So much so, they eagerly wanted to know what great Rabbi had taught this well-informed lad. The new revelation in the statements He had made absolutely astounded them!

It is my personal belief at the age of understanding, at eight years of age, Jesus knew he was called to be the Messiah and King of the Jews. Through the Holy Spirit, I think he was already conversing with God at this tender age.

Let us say that from eight to thirty Jesus lay in bed and talked with His pappa in heaven and grew in wisdom and knowledge. So when he is in ministry under the weight of massive healing and teaching and growing a following he used to go out early in the morning to spend time with daddy. Before any Peters and Johns where up asking him questions He used to pour out his pain and rejection and lowliness out to his Father and the fact that He simply could not heal all the sick on earth all by himself. Every day he set many free of disease and every day closed with questions and answers with his disciples till sometimes 2 am. Sometimes Jesus didn't go to bed and poured out his tears and prayers to the Father and his father would build him up and re-fill him and give him the anointing power for the next day.

As powerful as Jesus was he could not do a day without a few hours with papa. He had papa show him visions of future things and over the next day he saw himself doing what he saw in the vision that morning or night before. In this way Jesus only did what he saw His Father doing though him in the visions.

If Jesus with all his anointing that allowed him to heal 100% of the people that came to him and the ability to preach such profound parables needed the Father each day, what makes us think we can do anything without doing the same?

Kingdom Nugget 8
Crucifying His Flesh

Some Christians wrongly assume that the suffering of Jesus occurred just before and on the Cross itself. But Jesus lived with suffering long before His crucifixion and its associated agony.

The Apostle Paul, in the Book of Romans Chapter six, in the New Testament, talks much about "crucifying" the flesh. This term in Romans lines up with the words spoken by Jesus to His disciples, that to follow in His footsteps, they would have to first deny themselves, take up their cross and follow Him. Taking up one's cross would involve living in self-denial.

Back then as it is today, self denial is not something any generation really wants to embrace. Most people don't have a good understanding of "taking up one's cross" each day. To those that do continually have their cross weighing heavy on their shoulders, please accept my humble apologies. May God's grace super-abound to you for that costly decision.

Not many people may realize, but one major decision by Jesus would have been to leave his mother. For a young Jewish male to opt out of His cultural duty, as the older son of a widow, Jesus would have been a source of much negative gossip and would have possibly bought shame to his family. We could picture these gossips saying: "Mary, why has your boy deserted you? Why has your older boy neglected you? What excuse has He given you Mary?" Curious and outraged outsiders would have asked all these questions and more.

Although not having the official title of Rabbi, Jesus was recognized even in His teen years as a budding Rabbi by those who listened to His teaching.

At the required age of thirty, Jesus publicly began His short three year ministry. His first task was to choose His twelve disciples. Being led by the Holy Spirit, He mostly chose simple uneducated fishermen and even a hated tax collector to be part of His close knit team of twelve male students.

To others, Jesus would perhaps seemed to have laid down His natural human wisdom in choosing His disciples. God's ways are different to the ways of man. The criticism of man didn't worry Jesus in the slightest.

As Christians, sometimes, we too, must be willing to *become a fool for the sake of the kingdom of God!* Paul later confirmed in Corinthians 1:26-27 that God doesn't call the noble to do great things, but He calls the so-called "foolish" so that they might bring glory to God.

Every step Jesus took, including allowing a prostitute to kiss his feet and wash them with her tears; or choosing women to join His disciples; or by angrily taking a whip to the temple merchandisers, not just once but twice, all that Jesus did, he did in submission to the will of the Holy Spirit who was continuously calling the shots to glorify the Father.

Jesus was radical but He was authentic and real. He was one of the many believers who have gone before, who have displayed "out of this world" levels of humility. For only the humble can lay down the needs and wants of their own flesh and be crucified unto the Lord's will.

Kingdom Nugget 9
Salvation

Ask a variety of people about how they came to know Jesus and acknowledge Him equal to God the Father in Heaven and you will hear a variety of stories. Just as each of us are unique in character and circumstance, we all have our own special story about how the Lord Jesus made Himself real to our human spirit and how we finally surrendered our life to Him. This story is called our personal testimony and it always makes Satan squirm.

The day that we surrendered our life to Jesus Christ will always remain the most important day of our life - some of us were old enough to remember every detail. Some people, like me, were quite young and perhaps parts of the detail of your experience have been somewhat lost throughout the years. Regardless, the angels in Heaven rejoiced at a person's salvation.

People talk about miracles and all sorts of signs and wonders in the work of the Kingdom. We hear great stories of miraculous modern day healings, but I believe that all born-again believers have already personally experienced the most radical miracle of all. The day we decided to put our lives into the amazing hands of Jesus Christ the Lord was our greatest miracle ever! Exactly what occurred that day in the spiritual realm totally outstrips everything else that has been a milestone in our life.

Therefore, pastors in individual churches from every Christian denomination should have as their main priority within their church, the salvation of souls. Just as important, having a way to reach out to the local community and to bring new sheep into the Kingdom of God should be something each and every church leader should keep high on their agenda.

On a personal note, I came to know Jesus when a gifted Children's Evangelist came to our country Baptist Church. I remember, he sat us down and shared with us how we could forever have a wonderful close Friend. This amazing Friend would come into our hearts and would remain with us all of our lives, even to the day we die. Then, He would take us to live forever in a mansion in God's Heaven - this news certainly gained my attention.

I remember that I was so excited to hear about this wonderful Friend that I couldn't contain myself. I'm sure children today are still the same. Just like I was at the tender age of eight, I firmly believe that even young children do want to know about spiritual things.

My life has seen many hard times and much of that hardship has been self-inflicted. But other hard things in my life have not been my fault. I have experienced much pain, but at forty-six, I still acknowledge that the Lord Jesus Christ has been my closest and most loyal Friend throughout it all. He has never deserted me, for which I am forever thankful.

Kingdom Nugget 10
Continuing Salvation

There is a biblical term called "sanctification" which essentially means the continuing process of being saved. Scripture teaches that at salvation, *we were saved, yet, we are being saved daily and one day, we will be fully saved.* Salvation is therefore, a past, present and future work of the Holy Spirit in us.

Our spirit and our soul have called the shots up to the point of salvation, but now, every believer is to hand over the reign of their life to their born-again human spirit. Then, as we allow God's Spirit to rule us, the sanctification process will continue to change us to be more like Jesus. You see, at salvation, our temporary physical body and our eternal soul area were not changed. Yet amazingly, God now sees us as being perfect! That's because God is only looking at our human spirit, *which was made perfect at our salvation.* Therefore, one third of us can't be improved on in any way.

The body of every human being is only temporary, but the human soul and spirit are eternal. Therefore, God is very interested in our eternal parts more so than our fleshly body.

Every Christian's spirit is fully sanctified (meaning: set apart for God) but our soul too, is to be fully sanctified as well: it has to come under new management by learning to obey the promptings of our born-again spirit. Prior to salvation, we lived our lives by the directions coming from our soul area - that is, our personal thoughts and our emotions influenced our free will.

In our lifetime, we have all developed bad habits. We need to develop Godly habits and we can *if we allow* our born-again spirit to actually rule us. We all have issues to be dealt with, so the Holy

Spirit works in us with our cooperation, in what the Bible calls, "sanctification," which actually is the ongoing cleanup process occurring in our imperfect soul area.

God already knows what our soul will one day be like in Heaven. Therefore, at the moment of death, a believer's soul will receive the finishing touches of perfection, so that both our spirit and our soul can take their rightful place in Heaven. In the meantime, from salvation to that day of total completion, the sanctification process of God makes us more and more pure.

If we are growing in Biblical faith, we should be able to look back a few years and see a positive improvement in ourselves. As more years go by, when we look back to our day of salvation, there should be some definite evidence of ongoing spiritual growth in our soul area. The more we grow into being like Christ, the better our life is. The more we develop into an effective witness to others by our attitudes, behavior and decisions, the more we will resemble our perfected character in Heaven.

The wonderful thing is that we are forgiven and loved by Jesus, no matter what stage we are currently at, because God is relating to us by our born-again Spirit, which is perfect.

If we have been stagnant in our growth for years, God understands that. Therefore, if you are reading this and being stagnant is a concern to you, I pray that God will grace you with the power to move on and kick any annoying habits.

Kingdom Nugget 11
Your Life's Purpose

We all know that our life is to have a purpose, but unfortunately, not everyone is aware of what their purpose is. Because some people are consumed in knowing why they exist, or what is coming to them in the future, they may even seek a clairvoyant to find out their life answers. However, the Bible warns us very strongly that believers are not to seek information from this particular source. A pastor or prophet of God can much better assist you in this way. Seeing a clairvoyant is definitely not God's will for anyone as it opens the door to opposing evil spirits.

Many believers don't even realize that they can seek God themselves with their pressing questions. God delights for us to seek Him and to ask Him about things that concern us. He is fully aware that living life without direction and purpose is not a fulfilled life. Personally, I find much joy in now knowing that I was born to be a writer and a prophet of God. I can testify that there's much personal satisfaction when you are participating daily in God's plan for your life.

Finding your purpose might not be as hard as you think. Many times, our purpose is closely aligned with our gifts. What are you good at? What do you like to do? What would you like to be doing with your life if you were given a chance to do it? The answer to these questions could very well be what you were born to do. Sometimes, you just have to pray and try and make the appropriate moves, so that a door is opened for you to go through.

For example: Many places allow people to do volunteer work these days. Perhaps you could get a foot in the door by volunteering in your chosen life purpose occupation. Be mindful that you may not recognize your own gifting, but your close friends will be able to give you some ideas on how they see your particular gifting. Ask them, because they may help you.

If you haven't yet had the opportunity to practice whatever you feel your life purpose is, I know one thing for sure. God knows why you are here and if you seek Him, He will make a way where there seems to be no way. God is very good at opening doors and He is very good at comforting tired and weary souls. If you don't know your purpose, just keep seeking God. Ask Him to share it with you in a dream, or though another person who says, "Do you know what you would be good at, you should do such and such."

As a person living in destiny and purpose, I can assure you that life becomes very exciting when you are actually doing what you are called to do. I pray that God will show every unsure reader His particular purpose for them over the coming weeks.

Heavenly Father,

I ask you on behalf for every reader of this book who wants to determine Your perfect purpose in their life, that they will soon be touched by You and given Your answer. Would you speak to their heart, or give them a dream that shows them, or have friends of theirs share with them, exactly what they should do with their life. I ask this in your Son's precious name, Amen.

Kingdom Nugget 12
Knowing Your Gifts

Everyone is born with natural abilities that are evident to themselves as well as to others. Simply applying their natural abilities helps them live out their life purpose and destiny. For example: someone who has a great ear for music may become a talented musician or even a conductor of an orchestra. People kind of just fall into their natural talents and abilities. Other people enjoy all forms of sports or are interested in all kinds of technology, etc. There are all sorts of abilities that God places in people. Therefore, none of us are exactly the same.

However, if a person is a believer, they not only have natural abilities, but God sees to it that they will receive certain spiritual gifts, which in His foreknowledge, He has already ordained for them. These gifts are described in the Bible, but a comprehensive list and description of these can also be easily found on Google. You just need to do a search for a "Spiritual Gifts" test. Knowing your spiritual gifts assists a believer to discover God's life purpose for them within the body of Christ.

My personal gifts include giving, encouragement, prophecy and teaching.

A gift that is not often asked for is the gift of poverty, but other people would agree with me that I have this unusual gift. I live very simply, because I have an easy ability to do without. I am always looking at different ways to use my money to advance God's Kingdom. I am just naturally happy to walk in this particular gift because I consider it to be an enjoyable and satisfying life. Because I know not everyone thinks like I do, I realize that it is a gift that God has given to me to use for His glory and He gives me the joy to do it.

Every week, I spend money on my projects of books that I am preparing for the body of Christ to read, and to do so, I eat very simply so I can afford the associated costs. This, I believe, is exercising my gift of poverty. It's no big deal for me.

Every week, I meet strangers in the streets of Sydney, Australia and God gives me a prophetic word for them that will encourage them. Apart from writing and teaching, from time to time, I am moved in my spirit to contribute to certain ministries or individuals. Because I have the "gift of giving" it is never a problem or chore but is in fact, enjoyable for me. Another way my gift of giving is employed is that every ninety days, I have the opportunity to give some of my books away on Kindle and I've seen thousands of people download my books this way.

I share these things not to boast, but to simply inform the reader that when you have spiritual gifts and you are aware of them, life is very enjoyable. As a prophet and teacher, I am excited when God inspires me to teach things like this series of Kingdom Nuggets.

I pray you will go and do a spiritual gifts test and start to walk in your gifts, for in that way, you will not only be fulfilling your own unique destiny, you will enjoy fulfilment in life.

Kingdom Nugget 13
Giving It All for Jesus

It's wonderful to live a life serving Jesus. It's a great feeling to wake up each morning and be directed by the Holy Spirit. There exists such a peace in your heart when you know all that you are doing is directed by the Throne Room of God. From the point of my salvation to where I am today, has been quite a slow process mostly due to my own wrong choices, but I am now happily cooperating with God in His sanctification process and life for me has never been better.

Serving Jesus through taking directions from the Holy Spirit is a good life. It's so rewarding to have your day's activities planned by the Holy Spirit. For example: I'm currently working on a number of books at the moment. One has to have the cover finished. One has to have the final videos transcribed and edited, the manuscript prepared and the cover done. Also, of course, the book you are reading now, Kingdom Nuggets. I am so grateful for the help of the Holy Spirit in all of my writing.

Over the next month, I will seek the Lord for three Kingdom Nuggets posts each day and if one day I wake up flat and not in the mood to write, and worship music doesn't inspire me to get going, then the days of writing are set aside. God knows what I can handle and between us, things get done.

Satan tries all the time to hamper us by burnout, but God doesn't expect us to be a robot. Therefore, we need to be cautious even when being led by the Holy Spirit to do a task. What do you think the Holy Spirit is calling you to do? Can you pinpoint something in your life that is stopping you from obeying the Holy Spirit? God wants to take possession of you. Will you let Him lead you to do what He wants you to do?

Kingdom Nugget 14
Laying Your Life Down

I was reminded of a Scripture verse that sums this subject up well. I will quote it in the easy to understand Message Translation. *"Don't love the world's ways. Don't love the world's goods. Love of the world squeezes out love for the Father. Practically everything that goes on in the world, wanting your own way, wanting everything for yourself, wanting to appear important, has nothing to do with the Father. It just isolates you from Him. The world and all its wanting, wanting, wanting is on the way out, but whoever does what God wants is set for eternity."* 1 John 2:15-17

Because I spoke about sanctification in Kingdom Nugget No.10, you will realize that a person doesn't become a Christian and immediately lay down all of their life to God. Most new converts are still caught up with the lure of the world and all its goods and services. In the flesh, we have spent our life adopting the world's ideas and seeking the things of the world. We sought popularity and loving acceptance by others in order to feel important.

The Apostle John, in the passage above, says that worldly thinking is contrary to God's will for His children. Therefore, having a life that is "Christ" focused is one that the "world-system" will never be able to grasp because they are poles apart. Not many Christian leaders seem to quote this passage. Perhaps, they don't want to offend their listeners. Even many pastors and teachers want to be popular. The Apostle John was not the only one you may consider extreme, let's see what the brother of Jesus said: *"You're cheating on God. If all you want is your own way, flirting with the world every chance you get, you end up enemies of*

God and His way. And do you suppose God doesn't care?" James 4:4

Ask yourself this question. Is it possible to have an iPhone 5 and a High definition TV and an iPad and all the modern conveniences and still not be serving the world and its lusts? I guess there are some people who do use all these things for the glory of God. God actually wants us to prosper in our business life and in every part of our life. However, I would be sad if people had all these somewhat expensive items at their disposal and they were not also giving to God for His Kingdom purposes.

Please hear what I am saying, I am not trying to place guilt on you. Everyone needs to examine themselves and see how they rate according to these Scriptures. God loves us and does not want the world and its ways to consume us and therefore, lead us away from a rich relationship with Him.

Do you think that if God directed you to let go of some precious things in your life, that you would be able to do so? Do you think that these verses have convicted you and you might need to change some of your ways? What changes do you think you can make this week?

Kingdom Nugget 15
You Are Important to God

Everyone on earth is special to God. Each one of us is unique and has a special purpose in this world. But as believers, we are all part of the Kingdom of God. As such, all of us have an important job to do for God. In fact, we were born to do that work. This verse speaks of it.

Ephesians 2:10 - *For we are His workmanship, created in Christ Jesus for good works, which God prepared beforehand that we should walk in them."*

The idea that the Lord has prepared the works that we should walk in before we were born is especially exciting to me. When you find out what works you are supposed to be doing, it is all the more exciting. Walking and moving in your destiny is something that will fill your heart with joy and satisfaction. The fact that God has prepared works for you to walk in means that He intends you to find out what you were created to do and He will encourage you and assist you to do those things.

We are not left to our own devices.

We are encouraged to walk with God through the Holy Spirit each day of our life. If you do not know how to be led by the Holy Spirit or to hear from the Holy Spirit, stay tuned as we are going to cover that subject in other nuggets. The Holy Spirit is to be our Counsellor and Teacher and He is very willing to help us in every area of our life.

I don't want you to think that if you are not walking with God, that is, if you are not being led by the Holy Spirit each day, that you are in some way less important to God. God loves us all and He has a great purpose in mind for all of us. He desires us to grow with Him each day and each year. He absolutely delights in you and wants only the very best for your life. He desires to speak to you and later, in this book, we will look at the topic of "Hearing from God." Suffice to say here, if you are a Christian, then God wants to help you grow closer and closer to Him each day of your life.

Do you hear from God? Do you know what specific "works" God has prepared for you to do? Are you doing what God has called you to do? Is there any help you need to achieve what God has in store for you?

Kingdom Nugget 16
God Wants Your Help

It may surprise you that God wants or needs our help with anything because we assume that God is all powerful and pretty resourceful and can do well without us. Nevertheless, the mystery of Him "needing us" still remains.

I'm quite sure that God could get by without me! In fact, I'm very sure that people could be influenced for the cause of Christ without my particular input, but what is so cool is that God has chosen to use me in the process of winning people to Himself. It's such an honor to be used by God; it's such a high privilege to be His mouthpiece and to actually influence various individuals and groups of people. His extravagant grace in all of this certainly never goes unnoticed by me.

Yes, it is true. God wants to use you in His plans. No matter what you bring to the table, no matter what your skills are, He wants to use you. Every day in all sorts of ways, people are being used to fulfil God's Great Commission. So many people, without even knowing it, are being used by the Holy Spirit each day to further the cause of Jesus Christ. You may not know how you are being used, but you can be sure if you are a Christian, then God is using you in one of His many plans.

Let us therefore be mindful today of Jesus and His ways in our lives. Let us pause for a brief moment and reflect on how we believe that we are actually being used by God. We can stop for a short time and thank God for the way that He loves us and uses us.

Question time: What do you feel that you would like to do for the Lord?

God Spoke to People In the Old Testament

Does God speak in an audible voice to His people today? Many people are of the opinion that God doesn't audibly speak to His followers today. These people assume because He has not spoken to them or their friends, that God doesn't speak today to anyone. This conclusion may be reasonable to assume given their knowledge and their experience, however, it is wrong!

Starting with Adam in the Garden, then Noah and continuing with Abraham and all the other Old Testament saints, we have a rich history of God talking to His people.

Abraham was a believer in God. He just knew in his heart that there was a God. Because of Abraham's deep faith in God, he was selected by Him to become the father of a new nation. This nation still exists today – it is the Jewish nation. Because of his simple childlike faith in God's goodness, he was declared righteous – meaning he had right standing with God.

There were many Old Testament saints, so if God spoke to these saints before the time of Jesus and before the coming of the Holy Spirit, don't you think that He also wants to speak to you today?

God doesn't just speak to prophets, He wants to speak to all of us, but we are not listening. We don't hear because our minds are elsewhere or we don't think we are important enough for Him to talk to. God actually longs for a two way conversation with all of us. In fact, the Father, the Son and the Holy Spirit – all three members of the Godhead, really want to communicate with you personally. Over time, it's possible to identify the voices of all three. You can personally know all of them and you can know their personalities and the difference in their voices when you hear them speak to your heart/mind.

Because of the resurrection of Jesus Christ, the New Covenant is so much better than the Old Covenant. We should be hearing God speak to us easier and more often than the Old Testament saints heard from God.

Heavenly Father,

I pray that you open the spiritual ears of the people reading this. I pray as they ask you questions, that you would answer their questions right away in their heart/mind so they are convinced that You are speaking. Father, "speak" to your people, I pray and remove all doubts from them as You come into a deeper relationship with them. I ask this in Jesus' name. Amen.

Kingdom Nugget 18
Jesus Spoke to Paul

Most believers would know the story of Paul being knocked off his horse when he saw a vision of Jesus on his way to Damascus to persecute Christians. I believe that every young Christian, early in their faith, would have been told about the Risen Christ miraculously appearing to Saul, who later became the Apostle Paul. Jesus audibly and in much authority, convicted this devout Jewish leader, in no uncertain terms, that he was not to continue persecuting Christians.

Perhaps, not all Christians know that Jesus appeared to Paul, appeared in visions as Paul was going about his business as an Apostle of God's Grace. Jesus and Paul were very close. Although it's only mentioned about three times in the Book of Acts, which was a Book written by Luke, that Jesus appeared to him in a vision, I tend to think that Paul was walking with Jesus most of the time. You may remember that Paul actually went to Heaven on one occasion and this certainly would have impacted him big time.

If Jesus often spoke to Paul and appeared in visions so much that Paul actually spoke of it three times, don't you think Jesus would want to speak to you also and possibly appear to you in visions as well?

Before the Cross, Jesus actually promised His disciples that they would not become orphans after His death. Let's look at what Jesus said:

"I will not leave you orphans; I will come to you. A little while longer and the world will see Me no more, but you will see Me. Because I live, you will live also. At that day, you will know that I am in My Father, and you in Me, and I in you. He who has My

commandments and keeps them, it is he who loves Me. And he who loves Me will be loved by My Father, and I will love him and manifest Myself to him." John 14:18-21

Jesus kept His promise to His disciples. He only returned to Heaven ten days before the Day of Pentecost. This particular celebration was an annual Jewish Feast celebrated fifty days after Passover. Jesus later appeared to Paul many times and He spoke to him all the time.

Catch onto this type of faith and let Jesus speak to you today.

Kingdom Nugget 19
Holy Spirit Teaches Paul

There isn't a lot of information about it, but once converted, Paul went away by himself and was taught by the Holy Spirit the doctrine of the New Covenant. As a former scholar, Paul was no stranger to being taught something, but this time, his teacher wasn't a man, this time, he was instructed by the Master Teacher Himself: the Holy Spirit.

If we are ever in a place where we are afraid that the Holy Spirit cannot teach us, we have Paul's example that this is indeed possible. Paul, who for many years was taught in the desert line upon line, doctrine after doctrine, was a forerunner of many saints who have gone away with their Bible and have gone to a quiet place to be alone with God.

Many of us run to books to read, afraid that the Holy Spirit isn't good enough to teach us what the Word is saying. Many of us do not think we are capable of working out what the Scriptures are saying. These thoughts are not based on theory. Many of us have tried before to search the Scriptures and have found them dry and not forthcoming when we looked at them. It is my prayer that this will not be my experience or your experience and that the Holy Spirit will continually imbue the Scriptures for us.

Heavenly Father,

Please give us the confidence to be able look into your Word and to learn new things from You. Increase our understanding of Your Word by Your Holy Spirit and teach us Your ways Lord, I ask with faith. In Jesus' name, I ask. Amen.

Kingdom Nugget 20
Apostles Confirm Paul's Findings

After a long period in the desert, over ten years, Paul went up to Jerusalem to seek out the apostles and to share with them the things concerning his new faith and what he had discovered in the Books of the Prophets and the law (The books of the Law were the first five books of the Bible called the Torah). When he found his friends and shared these things, there seemed to be no major problem with what he had found to be true. The apostles simply admonished him to look after the poor as well.

This is such wonderful news for all modern day Christians as well. We have Paul's example before us that we too, can totally rely on being taught the Scriptures by the Holy Spirit. If by faith, we are open to new things, the Holy Spirit will personally reveal the Scriptures to our own heart with fresh understanding.

God wants to talk to us! God wants to lead us and teach us things. I have to say that there is nothing quite as wonderful as personal revelation. You can receive revelation from your pastor, you can receive revelation from a book, but there is nothing like the Holy Spirit teaching you personally and directly from the Bible itself.

With so much information available to us these days, it can become quite a challenge to us. Many of us believe certain doctrines about different things and when we read the Scriptures, we filter out all that doesn't line up with what we have already decided to believe.

However, in order to have revelation and to be taught by the Holy Spirit, we have to approach the Bible with an open mind, willing for our beliefs to be challenged. Sure, the Holy Spirit has a lot of Bible to work with, and many Scriptures that He can illuminate to us without challenging our beliefs, but we must always be open to God to receive a transformation, otherwise, we can become almost unteachable and that's being prideful.

We are always going to have people who don't agree with us. People can even use Paul's writings to prove two opposing doctrines. The important point I want you to understand is that the Holy Spirit is still speaking today and He is still in the business of teaching those who are thirsty. God has not gone silent! He has much to say to everyone. It's not only possible to hear Jesus speak, but it is possible to hear the voice of the Holy Spirit as well.

Heavenly Father,

Open up your Heavens, dear Lord, over the reader. Let the Bible come alive for them and let it speak to them afresh. In Jesus' name, I ask. Amen.

Kingdom Nugget 21
Saints Heard Jesus

Jesus didn't stop speaking to people when His last apostles died, like many people preach and teach their flock today. Jesus has been alive all through the history of the church, speaking to those who sought Him by faith.

In order to know more about these saints, a person has to be open to catholic writers in many instances, as some of them were the people of faith for many centuries, despite persecution. The church hierarchy and some of its practices had major problems, but there were many wonderful saints within the church whom God mightily used to bring about the reformation.

One saint, I think, who lived in the 17th Century, was called Jeanne Guyon. Jeanne not only heard Jesus speak to her, but wrote a book sharing how you can create a discipline in your life so that you can hear Jesus speak to you. I used that book so that I could learn to hear sentences from Jesus. The book is called *"Experiencing the Depths of Jesus Christ"* and it's a book I have read three times.

Jeanne Guyon's writings have influenced many great men and women of God. She clearly heard Jesus speak to her and her books were ultimately burnt in France by the establishment. She was feared by those in power at the time, because of her influence on people. God never changes: He is the same yesterday, today and forever. Therefore, if Jeanne Guyon heard Jesus speaking to her in the 17th century, it is definitely possible that He still wants to speak to His people today and why not to you, my reader?

Another amazing saint that many Christians have admired was Sadhu Sundar Singh. This former Hindu had given up on life and his Hindu faith and was suicidal. He told God that he was going to kill himself on the 5am train if God didn't reveal Himself to him by that time. Just before he left to throw himself before the train, Jesus appeared in his room and the young Sundar was totally overcome.

Sundar gave away all he owned, lost his family because of his religious choice and became a travelling Sadhu (Holy man). He walked around India and trekked to Tibet with no shoes and no possessions, preaching Jesus to all he met and healing many people.

If Jesus spoke to Jeanne Guyon and Sadhu Sundar Singh, don't you think that He can do the same for you? It does not have to be saints in the past that have heard from Jesus, it can be your experience also.

Heavenly Father,

Please open up the readers' spiritual ears today. Teach them to ask Jesus questions and have Jesus speak to their hearts/minds with His answers until they are confident to speak to Him. I ask this in Jesus' name. Amen.

Kingdom Nugget 22
I Hear Jesus Speak

In summary: God spoke to Old Testament saints and He spoke to New Testament saints as well. Paul, in the New Testament, heard Jesus speak to him, and the apostles confirmed what Paul heard through the Holy Spirit. We have heard that saints through history have heard Jesus speak to them. It's therefore, not a major jump then, to hear that Jesus speaks to me also. He longs to speak to you as well.

When I was quite young, I used to hear Jesus speak to me with simple verses out of the Bible and little simple choruses being placed into my mind. This was Jesus speaking to me and redirecting my sad thoughts onto Him and His promises. I didn't really hear Jesus speak in sentences until I read Jeanne Gunyon's book *"Experiencing the depths of Jesus Christ."* It was when I put her teaching into practice that I was able to speak back and forth with Jesus.

I know it is possible to hear Jesus speak to you today, because He speaks to me most days when I take the time to speak to Him. There seems to be no limit to what He has to say. The Bible really comes alive when He speaks about it to you. In fact, life seems to have no limit to it when the Author of Life is communicating with you.

When the Author of Life is speaking to you, life itself takes on a far deeper meaning. Jesus once told me that He couldn't tell me everything about my future because if I knew all these things, there would be no room left for faith. Jesus is very wise and I still remember Him saying that to me. I believe it's natural for us to want to know things concerning our future.

To hear Jesus speak, you often have to "still the clutter" of life. You need to completely still your mind of thoughts, and be still before Jesus so He can speak to you. When you want to hear Jesus speak, you will be conscious of your mind thinking on all sorts of things. All of those thoughts have to be stilled. You find out very fast when you are doing this that your mind is a very real enemy of the things of God. When you have stilled your mind, you can ask Jesus a question and see what He says. I'm positive that He will have something good to say to you in His answer.

Heavenly Father,

I ask that you open the readers' minds to you. I pray that if they don't buy Jeanne Gunyon's book, that you will show them how to be still and to hear Your Son Jesus. Father, assist them to communicate to You and have Jesus speak to them. I ask in Jesus' name. Amen.

Kingdom Nugget 23
Dealing With Counterfeit Jesus

Do you realize that if there were no original bank notes, no one would bother producing a counterfeit note! It's the very existence of a genuine treasure that tempts a deviate person to produce a worthless counterfeit. In the same way, certain aspects of genuine Christian faith can also be open to deception.

In the past, I have personally been deceived in this way when I wanted to hear the voice of Jesus speaking to me. I discovered that there is a voice that comes from the antichrist spirit that pretends to be the "voice" of Jesus. This voice was so convincing that I was completely hooked for quite some time and I had been a Christian for decades.

The enemy's ploy is of course, to trip us up and lead us further into deception. Many people, when discovering this deception, may be tempted to "throw the baby out with the bath water" as the saying goes. But this negative reaction, of course, also comes from a wrong spirit.

Many people don't hear Jesus speak as they fear that a counterfeit spirit may try to fool them and it's this fear of deception that actually stops them from hearing from Jesus. I want to share with you some of the characteristics of the antichrist spirit that I have discovered.

*First and foremost - an antichrist spirit loves all forms of religiosity.

This evil spirit will appeal to your desire to be accepted and publicly recognized as being a "good Christian" person. More often, it will accuse you of not being "good enough" to be a genuine Christian. On two counts, it almost tripped me up; it was almost demanding me to go and read my Bible more often and also to pray longer prayers and more often. But I have personally discovered that the Holy Spirit gently urges me, He never *demands* me to do these good things. Instead, He gives me a desire to do them.

Jesus wants us to value His Heavenly rewards over the praises of man. Man judges by the outer appearance but God sees into our heart. Jesus delights in us for "who" we are and not for what we do. He said to not let people know the good things you do, but we are to tell people about God's goodness towards everyone.

*An antichrist spirit works against your born-again spirit.

A few times, I have caught this spirit at work, it was asking me to do something that I just didn't want to do. I didn't feel led to do it. I have found that when the Holy Spirit asks me to do even a hard thing, he gives me the necessary grace to do it. However, the antichrist spirit doesn't give you any kind of grace to do what it demands.

*The antichrist spirit loves to give us false hope!

One example could be the hope of being exalted in some way. This spirit may promise that something really great in your life is about to happen. Then, the time comes and goes and you feel let down. We need to know that the hope that Jesus gives us is sure and steadfast, this "hope" is like a firm anchor to our soul, so that it holds us through all the disappointments and storms in life.

Biblical "hope" was once explained to me by an Apostle, as a filling in a sandwich, which sits on a firm base called "faith" and is covered over with God's "love." So faith, hope and love go together as an ongoing source of spiritual nourishment for our soul. Hope is vital to the human soul: to lose hope is called hopelessness and this is a terrible condition. Therefore, God lovingly protects "hope" between *faith* in God's ongoing goodness towards us and His deep *love* for us overwhelmingly displayed at Calvary.

There would be more common traits of the antichrist spirit, but these three characteristics are the ones that I have personally been fooled by. One of the enemy's objectives is to confuse you so much and so often that you give up trying to follow the Holy Spirit. Every evil spirit actually wants you to "throw the baby out with the bath water!" That is: to throw out the genuinely precious things along with the unclean.

I think God allows this evil spirit to operate in our lives so as to teach us how to discern good from evil. Therefore, even though it's a pest, God uses it for our good by making us stronger. There is no way I am ever giving up on wanting to keep hearing the voices of the Godhead and I am becoming much better at discerning the voices compared to times in my past.

Heavenly Father,

I ask that you work with each person who is being deceived by a false Jesus voice. Give them better discernment and let them have patience while they work things out. I ask that You will minimize any damage and actually bring good from this experience, so that Your name is glorified in both their life and in the lives of others. In Jesus' name, I ask. Amen.

Kingdom Nugget 24
The Good Shepherd

"Most assuredly, I say to you, he who does not enter the sheepfold by the door, but climbs up some other way, the same is a thief and a robber. But he who enters by the door is the shepherd of the sheep. To him the doorkeeper opens, and the sheep hear his voice; and he calls his own sheep by name and leads them out. And when he brings out his own sheep, he goes before them; and the sheep follow him, for they know his voice. Yet they will by no means follow a stranger, but will flee from him, for they do not know the voice of strangers." John10:1-5,

Now, the question I have to ask is this: Are you a sheep? Is Jesus your shepherd? If Jesus is your shepherd and you are saved, this parable says that you should be hearing the voice of Jesus. If you are not hearing the voice of Jesus in your life, you can still be a sheep but you are not living in the fullness of what God wants you to live in. People may disagree, but Jesus was clearly saying that His sheep hear His voice and that He leads them.

There may be many reasons why you are not hearing the voice of Jesus in your own life, but when all is said and done, those reasons will not last if choose to address them. Jesus is real, He is really living in Heaven and He wants to talk to His people. He does not want people thinking that He cannot speak to them. For far too long, people have assumed that only very special people and prophets can hear the voice of Jesus, but this is wrong thinking. Jesus not only wants to speak to you, He wants you to respond to His voice!

Heavenly Father,

Please show the reader the reason why Jesus wants to speak to them. Father, I ask that You break down every barrier that blocks people from hearing the voice of Jesus speaking to them. Father, create a real desire in their heart to hear Jesus speak to them. In Jesus' name, I ask. Amen.

Are You Worthy for Him to Speak?

Many people who don't hear Jesus speak to them feel they are not worthy of this honor. I find often when it comes to the gift of prophecy, that people do not feel worthy of this either. Some people simply think they don't measure up to others. The problem with us is that we look at our personal failures and we think that Jesus is keeping record of them. Therefore, we think God only distributes His great gifts to those who are more worthy than us.

Let's work on that assumption: The Apostle Paul said that he was the chief of all sinners, yet this man wrote most of the Epistles in the Bible. He was used mightily by God and he spoke about God's gifts more than any other person in the Bible. He operated continually in his gifting. His conversion was spectacular and his ministry was even more so, because his relationship with his Lord Jesus was so very intimate.

How is any relationship developed? Only by developing personal intimacy – this requires two people being so comfortable together that they can talk frankly together about anything. That type of relationship is exactly what God wants to engage in with us because we are His kids.

For the purposes of this book, we have covered the parable of the Good Shepherd. We have established that you are indeed a sheep and so you have a right to hear Jesus, your shepherd. We have established that other saints all through the history of the church have heard from Jesus. It is your right, and yet, if you don't grab hold of this right, you could possibly go all through your Christian life without ever hearing Jesus speak to you.

Jesus was in constant two-way conversation with His Father and He sent His Holy Spirit to enable us to communicate with Himself, His Father and God's Holy Spirit. There are so many verses in the Bible that tell us we are worthy of the love of God.

The gift of hearing Jesus is open to every believer - we each need to firmly grasp this truth. We must accept that we are loved and precious to Jesus. I know that when I received revelation of how much Jesus really loves me and how awesome His grace is towards all those He died for, then I rightly concluded that Jesus wants a proper relationship with every one of us.

Heavenly Father,

You have made us worthy though Your precious Son, our Lord Jesus Christ. Your Son came and died so that we might communicate again with you like you originally intended in the Garden of Eden. Jesus has removed forever the sin barrier between You and man. Father God, I ask that you will touch every reader's life and give them a personal revelation that in Christ, they have been made worthy to hear from Heaven. If they are not already "in Christ," I ask that you will draw them to Yourself so that they may respond to Your awesome love. In Jesus' name, I ask. Amen.

What Does God's Kingdom Look Like?

Jesus stated what His Kingdom looks like in Mark 16:17-18. *"And these signs will follow those who believe: In My name they will cast out demons; they will speak with new tongues; They will take up serpents; and if they drink anything deadly, it will by no means hurt them; they will lay hands on the sick, and they will recover."*

It's a sad reality that this entire Kingdom sign is not thriving on earth. Many churches teach on the Baptism of the Holy Spirit and the resulting new tongues and yet the casting out of demons and the sick being healed is still quite rare in our churches.

A few weeks ago, we had a prophet come to our church and he had a word of knowledge about someone having a bad hip. My pastor Robyn responded and with prayer, her hip was healed. It's this sort of thing that should be regularly seen in our churches.

I go to another church where the pastor drives a bus and he regularly releases the healing power of Jesus onto a passenger in his bus. I look forward to a church where this Kingdom principal is being activated every time the church meets together.

I believe that Jesus wants us to heal ourselves and others. I believe most Christians have barriers in their belief for miracles and therefore no practical experience. Jesus really does want His Kingdom of Heaven to manifest on earth. When His disciples asked Him to teach them to pray in Matthew 6:9-13, He started His model prayer with *"Our Father in Heaven, hallowed be Your name. Your Kingdom come, Your will be done, on earth as it is in Heaven."*

Jesus wants us to catch hold of that! There are some people who have captured this mandate. There are people who walk in the miraculous, wherever they go to minister. I just look forward to learning from these people, so that I can heal others through the power of the Holy Spirit in me. I want to teach others to heal as well.

Many people are also in bondage to demons and they need an anointed believer to help free them from their bondage. This is needed in the church and is a vital part of the Gospel. Sadly well meaning believers preach very loudly that Christians cannot be demon oppressed or possessed. This is a sad state of affairs.

Heavenly Father,

I pray that correct knowledge of the gifts of healing and the ability to cast out demons will be made more evident in your church. I pray that you will impart these gifts to me, so I too, can impart the gifts and encourage others to do so. I pray for truth to be shed abroad about what your full Gospel entails. In Jesus' name, I ask. Amen.

Imagine a World
Like This?

People become offended by the lyrics of John Lennon's song called "Imagine" and yet, in all my life, I have not seen a better picture of a model world of peace that lines up so well, to that which is promised to us one day, in the book of Revelation.

Ponder these lyrics and simply imagine this world. This song was voted the most popular song on the twentieth century, so it is clear that not only Christians want this perfect world to manifest.

"Imagine there's no countries It isn't hard to do Nothing to kill or die for And no religion too Imagine all the people living life in peace You may say I'm a dreamer, but I'm not the only one I hope someday you'll join us And the world will be as one

Imagine no possessions I wonder if you can No need for greed or hunger A brotherhood of man Imagine all the people sharing all the world"

If we had no money, and no insatiable desire to build up all kinds of personal possessions, and the world lacked greed and selfishness, the world would be well on its way to being like this song promises.

Do you know that they have cafes and restaurants and movie theatres in Heaven? Do you know that every person has a job suited to them in Heaven and yet they don't receive wages? Everything you want and everything you consume in Heaven is free. So money is not needed and all the issues that come with having or not having money don't exist either.

Imagine if you will, people working in manufacturing who enjoy doing their work. There are no sweat shops paying workers next to nothing to produce our popular brands. Imagine the whole world being brothers and sisters under Christ? Imagine peace reigning and no wars or sin! That's the New Kingdom that we can look forward to one day. It will be so exciting when it fully manifests when King Jesus returns to set up His earthly Kingdom.

Heavenly Father,

Show us the way to live on this earth. Show us the wrong choices that we so easily make that affect other people in a negative way. Help us to live better and make better choices in our way of life, so that we become more like You. Help us to love all people even when they disagree with us. In Jesus' name, I ask. Amen.

Kingdom Nugget 28
The New Earth

Scripture records the Apostle John having a vision of a future event. *"Then I, John, saw the holy city, New Jerusalem, coming down out of Heaven from God, prepared as a bride adorned for her husband. And I heard a loud voice from Heaven saying, "Behold, the tabernacle of God is with men, and He will dwell with them, and they shall be His people. God Himself will be with them and be their God. And God will wipe away every tear from their eyes; there shall be no more death, nor sorrow, nor crying. There shall be no more pain, for the former things have passed away."* Revelation 21:2-4

Can you imagine a world with no crying, no pain, and no sorrow? It would really be a New World. This new and perfect world seems impossible when you think about it. It would most certainly be an act of God. Ordinary humans are not going to just stumble into such a world, as it can only happen because of an act of God. As believers, we certainly look forward to it.

As yet, I'm not sure who will be living in this new world. Do all believers who die and go to Heaven come back in their celestial bodies and come and live in this world? Do we go to Heaven and then come back to this earth with God, or do only special people come back to this earth? What sets these people apart, what makes them qualify to come and be part of this New Earth?

I have spoken to Jesus about the pain and suffering on this earth and asked Him how He copes personally within His heart having to watch from Heaven, all the sin on earth playing havoc? He told me that He looks forward to the New Earth.

So, we have John's wonderful description of a physical new earth that is going to exist where life is going to be perfect for humans. Therefore, if there is no crying or pain, then you would think that sin would not exist anymore.

However, the Bible refers to a short rebellion occurring at some time and having to be dealt with by God. I have heard it said that when the second and ongoing generations come along in the New Earth, some of the people born will not want to come under the authority of King Jesus. So, sin will still be activated by a person's free will choice, much the same as it does today.

This New Earth might be closer than we think. The end of this era might well be upon us and we could be in the final years before Christ's return. It is very good that we know Him and we know that His ways are perfect and beyond question.

Heavenly Father,

We look forward to this New Earth. Please send Your prophets to tell us more about it. Bring us into the knowledge of You and Your Son and about this new home and secure our peace in the meantime. In Jesus' name, I ask. Amen.

Being Salt and Light In This World.

It may of course be many years before the Lord brings us to the New Earth promised in the book of Revelation. Until He does, it's our ongoing task to be His light and salt in this present world. God is love. Until we understand and have an experience of God's love, it's hard for us to be His light to the world we live in. Being God's light involves many things such as:

- Having the love of Jesus for all mankind! This involves loving the desperate that beg for money in the streets. It certainly isn't turning your gaze and pretending you didn't see their plight.

- Being light is turning the other cheek when you have been offended. Being light is not only publically forgiving a person that would choose to be your enemy, but it's also including your enemy in your prayers at night.

- Being light is essentially letting Christ, through His Holy Spirit, possess you and influence all your actions and decisions.

Therefore, to be God's light in your area of influence, you must be submitted to Christ and be in partnership with Him in earth becoming like Heaven – that's His Kingdom's purpose.

This world is in deep darkness. Many people give no thought to life after death and if asked, they most probably would say they believe in God and will go to Heaven. They live from one day to another without much thought of life after death. They live for the next great movie, the next time they shop, and they strive for things that have no eternal value. They want to have the coolest possessions and look great: to be someone of importance. They all want to live significant lives, and yet, without their Creator in their life, they don't realize that they are like ships without a rudder.

Conversely, when we are walking in light, our healthy status comes from being a King's kid!

We know we are loved without measure and loved without cause. We know that there is nothing we can do to stop Jesus loving us. It's from this position of being loved, and knowing our purpose, that we can be a vessel of God's love to others. Because we possess Christ as our lover/King, we possess everything. We don't need to buy unnecessary possessions or to seek special titles in order to give our life meaning and purpose.

It's from this position of being loved and secure that we can be a light of direction in a world that lacks truth and meaning for life. As we live in contentment and fulfilment, people will actually envy our stability and may even ask for our life's secret, then, we can share our faith.

Salt does two things. It brings out the flavor of food and it is used as a preserver of food when there is no refrigeration. I know Jesus meant both purposes when he told us to be salt to the world. People in this world need to know there is more to life then the next movie and newest iPhone. People need to see people of God doing life differently! They are watching Christians. Being salt can involve big things and even little things, for example:

- Remaining calm during worrying or negative situations - people need to see a peace
  in you that they would like to possess.

- Not wasting time on the Internet in the boss' time, taking extended breaks, or spending time and the boss' money on making private telephone calls.

- Making wise choices by not joining in gossip at your workplace. People will soon notice that you don't talk negatively about others behind their back.

When other people participate in these kinds of things, they will wonder why you don't. There will eventually come a day when someone at your workplace will ask you why you are different. Then you can share your faith with them, because the seeds you have been planting will have taken root for the Holy Spirit to work in your work friend.

Being salt is being consistently different to the decaying moral standards of the world. People are noticing your behavior so it should stand out as different. You may think little things are not worth much and your stand for righteousness is not being noticed, but people do notice.

Heavenly Father,

We ask that you share with us more from your Holy Spirit how to be light and salt in this world. Lead us each day by your Holy Spirit to demonstrate Your love to this world in a way that it leads people home to you. Give us this coming week, an opportunity to share our faith with someone. In Jesus' name, I ask. Amen.

The Freedom of Grace

Most believers would be familiar with this key passage in Ephesians 2:8-9. *"For by grace, you have been saved through faith, and that not of yourselves; it is the gift of God, not of works, lest anyone should boast."*

In the past, I glibly recited this verse, but now, I find myself living it.

If you have been brought up in churches like I have, this verse will be known to you, but if you are living the reality of this verse in your life, that's a totally different matter. So many of us have a list of things that we mustn't do to be righteous, and we also have another list of things that we *must* do to please God.

Some of the things that religion tells us we should be doing regularly would include: reading the Bible, praying, going to church and giving to God. I agree with these things, because they are all good habits that God wants every Christian to engage in. However, my point is, these very things are also on the same list of things that can be classed as "self righteous works" that Satan and other people will use to condemn you. For example:

- If you're only reading your Bible half an hour each day, they will ask you why you don't read it for at least an hour.

- If you are only praying ten minutes a day, you will be told that prayer really should be much longer.

- If you are not attending a church once a week, nearly every Christian will warn you with Paul's words "not to forsake the gathering of the brethren!"

- If you are not giving to God, well who do you think you are?

My conclusion is: The works are all good but the condemning attitude stinks. Why? Because many people believe that if they do these things, they are being a "better" Christian than others. The problem is how much and how often are we to do these things? And when you are doing them all, there is always pressure to do more. Maybe one of my readers has been told by someone, "Surely you must know that these are the signs of a mature Christian?"

It's very hard to believe and accept that Jesus loves you just as much if you are not giving to Him, and not reading your Bible, and not going to church. I say that because at one time in my life, I was homeless and lived on the streets for quite some time. I will always remember certain homeless people whom I met, who had incredible relationships with Jesus that far surpassed many Christians I know and they weren't doing any of these "must do" things, as far as I know.

It's so hard to accept that we are loved without cause. It's even harder to accept the fact that Jesus loves us as much as He loves people who excel in all these "must do" things. We must rid our mind of its old patterns and teachings of the world. It is "who we are in Christ," and not "what we do" that is God's main priority. Yes, it's true if we are truly "in Christ," we will want to do the things that please Him, but not everyone is yet able to do that. It takes time for the process of sanctification to actually change old habits. Praise God that He knows that.

Jesus paid the ultimate price for us on the cross: He paid in full. That's why, in His final statement, He loudly declared: "It is finished!" Then, He surrendered His spirit to God and died. He had totally fulfilled the Law's requirement and beaten the devil forever, all for us.

If you think you understand the grace of God, I will give you something to ponder: if you had a man in your church who was addicted to pornography and who was also a practicing prophet in your church, giving prophetic words to people, would you tell this man to stop working in his gift until he sorted out his personal life? Would you think his sin would be tainting the words he was giving to people?

I want you to know that the measure of grace we enjoy is to be the same measure of grace we extend to others.

I personally know a prophet who was addicted to porn for many years and he was also giving accurate prophetic words to others, with the permission of his pastors. I know this man because it was me. God had a big work to do in my heart and in healing my emotional wounds, but He was still using me and gifting me to bless others in the congregation. To me, looking back now – that was extravagant grace, not only by God, but also by my two pastors who were fully aware of my addiction at the time.

Christians are so full of rules and regulations. We are quick to say to people that we don't believe in "religion" and yet, when people are converted, we weigh them down with things they have to do to be a good Christian. (That IS religion!)

We all really need to receive a personal and deep revelation of the *love* of Jesus! We have to understand that we are not judged or accepted any more or any less for any of our works. Faith in God's love and grace, demonstrated on the cross, has saved us and grace goes on keeping us.

In Heaven, there is going to come a day when our Lord Jesus will judge every *believer's works* since their salvation and this judgment will determine their duties and position in Heaven. This judgment on believers will *not* be for sin, because Christ atoned for our sin once for all time. However, until that day, endeavour to try to love others and extend God's grace to them to the same measure that He loves and graces you.

Heavenly Father,

Please give us more and more revelation of your grace and show us through the lives of people that we know and who love us, what grace looks like. In Jesus' name, I ask. Amen.

What Love Looks Like

It's tempting to pull up the Scripture in 1 Corinthians 13 to share what love is, and I had that particular reference in my notes, but on reflection, I think we need to hear about an example of love that will illustrate it at a more personal level.

About five years ago, I met my former pastor's daughter. She was only twenty at the time and I was forty-two. When I first met her, she seemed reserved and I found out when I spent some time with her, that she was a very private girl. I was volunteering two to three days a week at our community center's kitchen, helping with the cooking of the meals for about eighty to one hundred men and women each day.

Sarah had been appointed as a temporary manager of the kitchen. I started to work with her and talk to her. When I say I talked, I mean, I talked and talked for hours! She never once told me to be quiet and to get on with my work. At that time, I had many weird ideas and beliefs concerning my particular role in God's overall End Time's plan, but she never tried to correct me, or tell me I was wrong. I spent hours and hours talking to her and telling her all about my life and slowly, she started to share her life with me.

To me, she was always patient, understanding and kind. She never ever judged me. She was such a good listener and had a way of questioning me to draw further information out of me. She would let me commence the same story for the third time, before she told me she had heard it before.

Today, I would like people to say these nice things about me!

However, back then, I had been known to impatiently cut people off if they started to repeat a story to me – that was so rude of me. I was egotistical and aggressive and far too talkative.

In due time, after a solid friendly relationship was built, she began to dispute with me about some of my firmest convictions. To assist in this, she used books that she had already read and employed various other methods for me to see the light.

I slowly came from a life of torturous legalistic thinking to a life of being loved by God's grace, all because of Sarah. One time, I had this huge argument with her and I thought she would never talk to me again. The next day, she was once again her loving self, just as though nothing had ever happened.

Sarah loved me when only my mother was able to love me.

I was an angry and argumentative "know-it-all" who could not be corrected. I was full of pride and very disturbed. I was so lonely that if someone would listen, I would speak non-stop for hours. I wasn't very loveable but Sarah made it her mission to love me and bring me some of her light. I cannot thank Jesus enough for allowing Sarah to come into my life. I am in tears as I type this. Sarah has moved on now, as God has other plans for her.

Today, I am no longer imprisoned by legalistic ideas and other old mindsets. Therefore, I am far more peaceful and loving. Today, I am very open to being corrected and will apologize when I think I have been out of order. I am not as prideful today, because I have finally developed a teachable spirit.

In reflection: Sarah was a "little" Jesus to me. It is far easier to talk the walk, than to walk the talk, if you know what I mean. Sarah could do both very well. God's love is being like "Sarah was to a belligerent man like me." I am living proof that a leopard can change his spots, but it took a lot of love from a very Christlike believer to do the job.

Heavenly Father,

Please bring to all of us a "little Jesus" to be our special friend and to show us Your love on earth. Thank you for Your grace, Lord and for nurturing us, so that You can gently lead us to Your truth and understanding of things. In Jesus' name, I ask. Amen.

Kingdom Nugget 32
Knowing Jesus

When Scripture speaks of the word "know" it can mean the "intimacy" that is shared by a married couple in sexual union. For example, Genesis 4:1 says. *"Now Adam knew Eve, his wife, and she conceived and bore Cain."* Therefore, I believe that when Jesus replied to a boastful person in Matthew 7:23 *"I never knew you, depart from Me,"* He was saying that they had never entered the bridal chamber with Jesus and feasted on His love.

Knowing Jesus is so rewarding. It's wonderful to lie in bed at night and chat to Him before going to sleep, and for Him to talk about what is going on in my life and offer His opinions. He confirmed that my current book is exactly what He wants me to publish. He assured me about my soon coming expenses and told me not to worry, it would be okay. He promised that I would always have inspiration to write the books that He planned for me. That was the essence of lasts night's conversation with Jesus.

I just love being able to have conversations with Him. Having the ability to converse with Him about so many subjects overwhelms me at times. I am always asking questions and Jesus always answers them. He is happy to talk on all sorts of things happening in the world. We have conversations about what He thinks of our world leaders and the current investigations into paedophilia in the church. Just being able to watch the news on TV and asking Jesus for His comments on what is true is so amazing.

One time about fifteen years ago, I asked Jesus to share some of His worries and pain with me. I told Him I was always sharing my life with Him and I thought it was time He shared His life with me. I didn't know what I was really saying at the time, and when He started to share His feelings and what He cries about in

Heaven, my life at that time, went very dark for many years. I didn't know then, that I was being prepared to become a prophet, but since Jesus has been sharing His heart with me, we have become closer friends.

God is God and He can do anything, but it's not His will to do everything. For instance: He refuses point blank to override man's right to exercise his own free will. Therefore, our bad choices sadden the heart of God, because He loves us all so much. Most people don't think about sadness or pain in Jesus' life. They are so caught up in their own life and worries that they presume that God has it easy in Heaven. Knowing that He does suffer pain might change your prayer life!

Jesus comes down to visit me a lot. One time, I asked Him why? He said that He has always been with me every day but I just don't acknowledge Him every day. I asked Him for a Scripture and He said: *"And lo I am with you always."* He always surprises me.

Many times I go to Heaven at night when I speak to Jesus. It's another realm and quite an extraordinary life to be in Heaven so often. But if you had a good friend, wouldn't you visit His house also, and not expect Him to come to your house all the time?

Knowing Jesus gives me much to write about and plenty to sing about when I worship Him.

One day, I was in church and Jesus asked me to bow down on my knees during worship and so I did. As soon as I knelt on the carpet and put my arms in the air, Jesus knelt down beside me and worshipped His Father with me. When I got used to Jesus worshipping next to me on His knees, we were caught up into the throne room and were both before the Father's throne on our knees worshipping. Before the host of Heaven, the King of Kings was on His knees worshipping His Father and He took me with Him!

This was one of my all-time favorite visions of Heaven and it all came from me obeying Jesus and getting down on my knees.

I have proved in my own life that one of the keys to a close walk with Jesus is "obedience." I cannot stress this enough. When Jesus, your Friend, wants you to do something, you should just do it! God knows what is best for us and even if things seem hard to us, they are only hard for our flesh. Our "flesh" includes the physical part of us and also it includes our soul area. Jesus wants our flesh to be subdued by the Holy Spirit in us. When it is, we will be walking with the Holy Spirit. (This is actually walking with Jesus.)

One time, Jesus asked me to do a waltz during the church worship time. I was to dance as if He was in my arms. Totally embarrassed, I walked to the isle and with my arms in a dance position, I began to slowly waltz and then, Jesus came and stood in my arms and we were both waltzing!

As soon as I relaxed and got my dance right, we were then taken to the throne room and once again we were dancing in front of the Father, right in front of the host of Heaven. Both the worship on my knees and the dancing in Heaven would not have happened without me first obeying the words of Jesus.

Heavenly Father,

Bless the readers as they read these Kingdom Nuggets. Speak deeply to them and let them have all the keys to a close relationship with You and Jesus. In Jesus' name, I ask. Amen.

Kingdom Nugget 33
The Surrender of Your Will

One thing I do have is a strong mind. Even with a mental illness, my mind is like a bull: it runs and runs and it's very powerful. Therefore, stilling my mind so that I can talk to Jesus is a discipline that I have had to learn. As soon as I talk to Jesus, my mind takes off and thinks about other things.

My mind in my soul area is like every human being, it is full of selfish thoughts. I may see myself as being very spiritually minded and yet, when I want to be my most spiritual and talk to Jesus, my mind instantly rebels and tries to distract me. Because we allow all sorts of garbage into our mind, we all need to have it renewed each day by Jesus.

I mentioned previously, in the "knowing Jesus" nugget, that I watch the news on TV. I have to say that I don't do that very often. We need to keep informed, but I find the news is mostly full of bad news. When I said we take in garbage every day, the items in the daily news are often part of that garbage. To surrender to God, we have to let certain things go, that our flesh enjoys. That's what the word "surrender" means: it's giving up in a battle and passing self-will over to a new authority.

We have God's assurance that there is a real battle for our life and our attention. It's not possible to fully surrender to Jesus in one go. Surrendering to the Holy Spirit's will, is a moment by moment personal decision to do things God's way and not our own fleshly way. We need to be aware of what God wants and to be prepared to continually let go of anything that's not of God.

Jesus wants all of you! He has your spirit, but He also wants to have control of your body and soul: He wants the very best for the whole person: He wants you to have a healthy active body and a healthy active mind. He wants you to have His heart and to do all things to the best of your ability. In summary: He wants you to constantly ask for His help and include Him in all your decisions.

Therefore, we need to hear Him and obey what He is saying quietly to our spirit. Many things He asks us to do will not come easy to our flesh. In fact, you could even do some things for God for years and they would never become easy for you. I'm sure a Christian nurse never gets enjoyment from cleaning up soiled bedclothes, but as part of her everyday duty, she does it graciously.

God is after us: He is pursuing us: He wants all of us! He is never going to give up. We have given our lives to Him, so allow Him to take up His rightful place and rule. He will still work within the confinements of our self-will and will never force His wishes on us. Therefore, crucifying the flesh has to be a daily moment by moment decision on our part.

Heavenly Father,

Take me, I am yours. Teach me to submit to you and lead me each day into more and more surrender. I ask this solemnly. In Jesus' name, I ask. Amen.

Kingdom Nugget 34
Humility

We are exhorted/encouraged in Peter *"to humble ourselves under God's mighty hand and in due time he will lift us up."* *1Peter 5:7*

Many people know of this Scripture. Even though I can quote it, I have to admit that I have no idea how you achieve this in one's life! How does one go about humbling oneself?

I know that humbleness on my part will in time cause God to lift me up. I know that I have to wait on Him to promote me and give me speaking engagements. I have been waiting patiently and sometimes, not so patiently, to be invited to speak in pulpits. In the last couple of years, this burning desire has been somewhat relieved, as three pastors have written to me for permission to use my book "The Parables of Jesus Made Simple" as a weekly Bible study. I am therefore quite excited that in one way, I am speaking in three churches each week.

I guess I can humble myself by continuing being a friend of my pastor and encouraging him in all he does, rather than pestering him for another speaking engagement.

Perhaps being humble is being on Facebook knowing that you are a prophet, but not having your Facebook name *Prophet* Matthew Robert Payne. Perhaps humility includes not putting your Facebook name as *Apostle* such and such!

But as to humbling myself when I was very prideful, I had no clue whatsoever about that! I didn't recognize pride in my life and would become really angry at people who dared to suggest I was proud. Like a typical Jezebel, I spoke about myself too much. In fact, I seemed to think that the universe revolved around me and the things I was going to do.

I never did humble myself, but God humbled me big time!

God humbled me through four years torture, and through a friend giving me a good book on the grace of God. These years of torture were a fiery trial. They were a major chastisement from the Lord. It says that the LORD God disciplines those that He loves and He simply was running out of time with me. I needed to be brought low to the ground.

I was so full of myself. I had written hundreds of articles on Ezinearticles.com and in many of them, it was not God getting the glory because they were all about me and how good I thought I was. I couldn't be corrected in any way and was quite abusive to anyone who dared to try and correct me or point out that I was wrong.

I believed in a very angry God for so many years. Yet, even though I was addicted to prostitutes at the time, I still considered myself to be a very obedient and holy person! I did not humble myself in the slightest. Thankfully now, I have been made to see things in a different way. I now fully embrace God's Word that says: *"God resists the proud but gives grace to the humble."*

Moses, who was a leader in the Old Testament, was said to be the meekest/most humble man on earth. But I find it quite amusing that it was Moses who actually penned those words about himself. Yes, of course I know it was the Holy Spirit that had inspired him to say these words as it was obviously a correct statement. Meekness is defined as great power, under the authority of a much greater power.

Jesus said He was "gentle and lowly in heart" and these qualities call for meekness and humility. God the Father, God the Son and God the Holy Spirit, are all equally powerful. Yet, Jesus on earth, in order to identify Himself with man, actually became one of us, except He was born sinless. He had to totally and continually submit Himself to the authority of His Father's will for Him in every situation.

Moses demonstrated the same commitment: he was totally submitted to God's directions. Moses was sent by God to the Egyptian Pharaoh and ultimately freed up to two million slaves with a "stick" that was anointed by God! Such was his anointed power and authority and such was his humility that he simply obeyed God and did all the crazy things God said to do and say. Our sick world today needs someone like Moses.

Moses had such a good relationship with God that we read in Exodus 32:12 that he even confronted God's anger by saying to Him, *"Turn from Your fierce wrath"* and in verse 14, we read, *"So the Lord relented from the harm which He said He would do to His people."* God was often angry in the days of the Old Covenant but on the Cross, all of His anger against all mankind was poured out onto Jesus. God may be grieved at times, but He is not angry anymore with anyone.

I have now met six apostles. Because of their meekness, each of them had a lot of time to hear me share my life and stories with them. Each of them had a powerful anointing on them that allowed them to preach for an hour and never let a person tire of the sermon. Each of them was a servant and considered their role was to lift up the body of Christ. Each of them took me under their wing and spoke to me as a son and a friend.

Each of them had me totally captivated. I would listen in to their conversations with others, simply to hear them speaking. All of them exercised the gift of healing and often, they heal more non-Christians than Christians. They all said that some Christians let their beliefs override faith when it comes to personal healing, but an unbeliever is free of religious hangups and will simply reach out and be healed.

Each of them brought gentle and inspiring correction to me, because they were anointed to speak the correction the Holy Spirit was telling them to show me. A true apostle doesn't boast, he teaches through example. I'm blessed and happy to have an apostle in my life every week. I am so excited to be around someone I want to emulate.

If you want to learn humility, place yourself around people who are humble and learn from them. I wish you well.

Heavenly Father,

Please show the reader what true humility looks like. I ask that You bring a humble brother or sister into their life, so the reader can see true humility demonstrated. Father, show them Your grace and mercy and mould them into who You want them to be. Draw them into Your loving arms. In Jesus' name, I ask. Amen.

Kingdom Nugget 35
Love

What does love look like? According to Misty Edwards, an anointed singer and worship leader, love is Jesus hanging on the cross, looking at you with extravagant love in his eyes, full of Divine mercy and compassion. Jesus in His living, in His loving and in His dying, was what love is. He continually showed us what love is and what love does!

The Pharisees cunningly brought the woman caught in adultery to Jesus, in order to have a reason to convict Him if He forgave her, but Jesus saved the woman's life, by showing her the grace of God.

Sure, Jesus answered the religious leaders in a way that they could not argue with. Jesus broke their understanding of the law at the same time, but on that day, there was far more to it than Jesus being right and them being wrong. In every generation since, WE (male and female) WERE THE WOMAN! Yes, I said it, we were that woman.

"I have never been an adulterer!" I hear you cry in objection. However, the Word says that we are all sinners - we are all guilty of doing and thinking things that require our eternal life to be spent in Hell. Adultery is just one of many sins. (Man, not God, grades sin.)

But whilst we were still sinners with no knowledge of God, Jesus, God's Anointed One from Heaven, died an agonizing death, naked on a cross of shame.

Jesus not only had the Pharisees put down their stones that momentous day when they accused us, (all sinners) but when the punishment for our sins was meted out forever, it was not taken out on us, but it was taken out on the actual body of Jesus, the Son of God.

Have you ever seen yourself as the woman caught in adultery?

I know I never had, until I felt inspired to write that. We also have to accept what Jesus said to that poor lady, *"Neither do I condemn you."* Oh, but the religious Christians will quickly quote the rest of the verse, *"Go and sin no more."* They will point out that every person has to be holy and spotless to get into Heaven. Yet, like the Pharisees, legalistic believers will weigh people down with heavy yokes of law and give them no solution or power to overcome their own personal sin.

As Jesus took the full force of the whip, time and time again, each time with its metal inserts ripping his flesh from his body, He endured it, according to Hebrews 12:2, *"with the joy that was set before Him."* As He suffered the excruciating pain of each whip stroke, He was thinking of all those who one day would respond to the Gospel Message and surrender their lives totally to Father God and the joy of having many brothers and sisters, sharing in God's loving care in Heaven.

Some people say that Jesus on earth was an angry person. This opinion comes from the fact that Jesus had angrily taken a whip to the Temple salesman and He also rebuked the Pharisees. These people don't understand what happened after the Temple scenario. After Jesus rose from the dead, many people of Jerusalem discovered that He was in fact the Son of God. They then understood that the radical clearing of the Temple was a fulfilment of the Scripture that said the zeal for his Father's house would burn within God's Anointed One.

Has someone ever torn strips from you with their words? Have you ever provoked someone who had been holding back their pent up anger for a long period and then, you received months of their pain leashed upon you? I have.

Often, what they say isn't easy to hear, and yet it can be very illuminating to you. You can learn much from such an outburst if you are really interested in seeing past their anger and really pondering the truth of what they actually said.

The same was true of some of those Pharisees. They had received the strongest rebuke of their life from Rabbi Jesus that day, when the woman was caught in the act of adultery and was being judged. Up till then, the Pharisees had displayed wisdom and had received favor with most of the Jewish people.

Jesus' words, oh yes, they were not pretty, but they had such a strong ring of truth to them, that some of those guys actually repented years later, as the Apostles taught on the Risen Christ. Sure they may not have left their profession to join the growing sect called Christianity, but I know that a few of them became secret followers of Jesus.

Even in His justified anger, Jesus had issued His rebuke with love, in the hope of turning a few of them that weren't too proud.

Of course, this is all extra knowledge that Jesus has told me, but what other reason did Jesus have at that time? Jesus was humble and He didn't need to rebuke them, unless it had a redeeming effect, not only on the woman, but on all the witnesses and revengeful accusers gathered that day.

With the two Temple clearings and the rebukes of the Pharisees aside, Jesus was a man who was the absolute expression of love. He was God in human flesh. If you have a problem with loving yourself or others, you don't need to read the "Love Chapter" in Corinthians again, you simply need to draw closer to Jesus and learn to obey His Spirit and manifest His heart more and more each day that you live.

Heavenly Father,

Lord, let my readers know of Your abundant grace. Lead them into your light and show them your Son's face so as to cause His glory and love to overwhelm them. In Jesus' name, I ask. Amen.

Kingdom Nugget 36
Practical Salt and Light

When you surrender your will and your life to Jesus; when you have grown to know Jesus really well; and have become humble; and you have learned to love as explained in my last three chapters, you are ready to be the practical "salt and light" to the world that you live in.

In the previous chapter, I mentioned that we represent the women caught in adultery. I now want to show you how many of us are still adulterers. We need to understand this repent of this behavior as it will seriously impede our effectiveness as salt and light in the world.

"You lust and do not have. You murder and covet and cannot obtain. You fight and war. Yet you do not have because you do not ask. You ask and do not receive, because you ask amiss, that you may spend it on your pleasures. Adulterers and adulteresses! Do you not know that friendship with the world is enmity with God? Whoever therefore wants to be a friend of the world makes himself an enemy of God." James 4:2-4

This is pretty serious language from the brother of Jesus, one could call it a rebuke. James does not mess around in his epistle. We all know what lust is in the sexual sense: it is not a good form of love: it's a perversion of what is right and good.

Lusting is our insatiable desire to have all that we can. Today, in the modern world, a person may want a laptop, a high definition TV and a smart phone. Many people in the world lust for the most expensive things this world can offer. Even when they can't afford it, people will still lust over such temporary things as brand name clothes, a smart and sexy looking car, and a luxurious home to live in.

In the West, we allow murder and slavery in other countries to exist, so that we can get our best brands of coffee, chocolate, Nike, Apple products and so on. When governments can't get control of oil, they are likely to go to war.

James says in verse three, that we often do not have because we do not ask God. I'm not guilty of that one, as I rarely ask God for anything. The second verse is more the point. You ask and do not receive because God knows you will spend it on pleasures and luxuries and not for needs. God doesn't want His children to be like the people of the world: selfishly full of lustful desires for temporary treasures.

God calls those in His church, who are caught up in this world's lie, adulterers and adulteresses! So many Christians that cry poor have in their possessions, expensive things that are really not essential. They cry poor, because they want more and more and more of the world's attractions.

Jesus says, through his brother, that we make ourselves whores if we behave like that. We are committing adultery on Him. He is no longer our first love! He has been relegated to a "bless me God" and servant of our lusts and desires. He says if we are like that, we are acting like God's enemy and not like His children.

I have to ask you, how many enemies of God will enjoy Heaven? To be an enemy of God is not good, unless of course we repent and change our ways. We need to seriously respond to God's love and grace displayed on the cross of Jesus. When all our money is tied up in the things of this world, we haven't any left to give to others, or to contribute to the building of God's Kingdom work.

A man I know died and went to Heaven and came back twenty minutes later totally healed. He travels around various churches, sharing his story and saving skeptics. I once saw an atheist friend of mine get seriously rocked when I played this man's testimony in a boarding house in the early hours of the morning.

This "miracle man" who had died, travels around the country and as he shares about his short trip to Hell and Heaven, people kept asking him if he saw the mansions up there and what did they look like? So many people had been asking this same question. One day, being very disturbed, he asked Jesus, why are people so interested in the mansions of Heaven?

Jesus told him it was a personal desire here on earth, so they really wanted a big mansion in Heaven as well. This really upset this man and it upsets me as well. I have been to my house in Heaven a few times and it is by no means the greatest mansion. It's certainly a grand mansion compared to my very modest Housing Commission apartment and it gets me very emotional every time I go there.

There are so many people who genuinely need financial help. If you live in a big city like Sydney, you would see the homeless. I know religious people have reasons why they don't give them their money, but they could still ask them if they wanted a nice, cold Coca Cola. You'll be surprised how many would be thrilled about such an offer.

There may be a single mother in your church with only one income and a child or children to look after. She could do with a trip to the clothing stores and you buying her children some nice new clothes. She would not be able to repay you, but your Father in Heaven will see the things you do in secret to others and He will reward you.

Most likely, there would be a homeless shelter in your area. Normally if they serve a free drink, it will be a cheap, watered-down cordial. Perhaps, you could purchase boxes of soft drink when they are on special and contribute to a hundred homeless people being extravagantly blessed as they enjoy their midday meal at the center.

Alternatively, these shelters don't serve steak. Perhaps instead of updating your iPhone, you could use some money to provide these sad and lonely men with a much appreciated steak meal. Perhaps if you are bold, you could even convince your friends to help you raise money for a special party at the shelter one day. You could give them this treat as a way of expressing God's love to them. People need to know that Christians have the love of God in them and to show that love in a tangible and humble way.

Ask God for direction in these matters. I guess being homeless for six months always has me pleading for these wretched souls. You may not have much money, but even without money, you could volunteer at a homeless shelter and simply listen to the stories of these sad people.

Listening is a wonderful gift that can be easily used to bless others. After a time, when they have talked their lonely hearts out for half an hour or an hour, they may ask you what prompted you to come and visit them. That is when you can share with them, that "Jesus can't make it today, but He told me to come down and make friends with people that could do with another friend in life."

I could go on and on about how you can be salt and light, but if I have convinced you in any way, make the change and you will be blessed.

Heavenly Father,

Have Your perfect way with these readers, I ask You in Jesus' name, Amen.

Kingdom Nugget 37
Faith for Miracles

This is one subject that I honestly do not feel qualified to write on.

However, I do know that to live the Kingdom life in its fullness, as the apostles did in the Book of Acts and also those who minister today in power, one must not only be able to speak about miracles but have personal testimony of them to show others God's mighty love. My Jesus is alive today and He wants to heal people though His children by the anointing of the Holy Spirit. Personal healings are the greatest testimony to the unbeliever that the Lord Jesus Christ, whom we adore, is alive and well.

I remember the first miracle that the Lord did though me. The person affected wasn't anywhere nearly as shocked as I was, when God had used me to do something miraculous. I was in an infamous red light district of Sydney, Australia. I was having a coffee with two heroin addicts who used to sell pot/marijuana each day to people passing by. These addicts had to continually support their illegal habit any way they could.

A prostitute came up to us who had a heroin habit and was moaning that she was getting really sick. Her body was in the painful process of heroin withdrawal. If a heroin addict goes without their drug for even a day, the pain in their body will keep increasing and seizures and other unpleasant symptoms will manifest in them. These nasty experiences will hold them in bondage for up to four days, unless they get their next shot of heroin.

My drug selling acquaintances had an addiction to heroin and cocaine, and that habit had them spending upwards of eight hundred dollars every single day to keep them happy and safe. The last thing they were going to do was to give some of the money they earned to this suffering girl. They had their own habit to support.

After a minute or so, I knew in my spirit that the girl's crying wasn't going to induce any compassion. I was getting cutup inside that I didn't have fifty dollars in my wallet to pay for her shot of heroin. I was crying inside and this girl was crying outwardly. I heard Jesus say to me. "Ask her if you can pray for her."

I could see that she was desperate, so when I asked her if I could pray for her, she immediately said "Yes please!" I asked the Lord Jesus "what should I do now?" Jesus said, "Ask her to move her hair away from her forehead, lay hands on her forehead and say the word 'peace' out loud."

I did what I was told and said, 'Peace.'

The girl rocked back in her seat and had her eyes closed for what seemed a long time but I guess it was only for thirty seconds or so. She then opened her eyes, leaned forward with her hands in the air as a loud question shot out of her mouth, "What is this?"

Without knowing what had happened, I simply said, "You are now experiencing the peace of God." She was so happy. No longer was she sick or in pain. She wanted to know how she could get this feeling again.

I had seen my first move of God.

That little miracle was birthed out of my compassion and love for her. I have been told that it is our compassion and our love combined with a proper understanding of the power we possess as a King's Kid that allows people to experience healing from an anointed child of God. On that day, I did not have faith for that to happen. I did not have the faith for a miracle, but I was begging God for an answer and He met my cry.

I have been told by people who move in the gifts of healing that it really all comes from love and not being afraid to stand in the gap for a person who is sick. God wants to use all believers as a living conduit of the power of the Holy Spirit. We simply haven't seen enough healings, or been around enough people who move in the gift, to have the faith that we could actually be used to heal someone.

Another time, I had an old friend of mine search me out at my church, because he wanted to speak to me and spend some time with me. As church finished, we walked into the city to buy some lunch at Burger King. As we walked, my friend confessed to me that he was in agony with back pain. He said that his prescribed painkillers were not strong enough and he was in constant pain. He said he wished God would heal him.

I put my arm around him and hugged him to myself and said, "You know I would heal you myself if I had the faith for healing." He told me that he knew I would and he just wished he could find a way to stop his back from hurting.

When we arrived at Burger King and were in the line Jesus said to me, "Ask him if you can pray for his back."

I asked him and he said "Yes." When he told me where it hurt, I laid my hands on him and asked God to take the pain away and to heal his back so that he would never be in pain again." Well guess what? That prayer healed him on the spot and it has been six years now and he has never had a problem with back pain since that simple prayer.

Once again, I did not have the faith for healing. I simply did what Jesus told me to do.

The third miracle happened when a ministry friend on the internet asked for prayer as she had been experiencing a constant migraine for seven years with no reprieve. When I received her email plea, I didn't pray for her and hit reply because I was too stunned. I was wondering how on earth was I to tell her that I lacked the faith for such a healing to happen.

Two days later, as I stepped off my train, I thought of her email and her seven year migraine. I knew that I only have to have a headache for two hours and I go crazy without painkillers. When I contemplated her being in agony for seven years straight, my eyes filled with tears of compassion and I started to weep for her situation. As I publicly wept and started to walk home, I began to shout out to God and plead with Him to heal her and to not allow that migraine to ever come back again. When I got home, I sent her an email to say that I had prayed for her and I hoped my prayer would come to pass.

The next morning, I received another email from her. In it, she said that when she began to open my email, before she could even read it, she was knocked to the floor under the anointing of God. As she stood to her feet, the migraine left her! That was a year ago and she has not experienced another migraine.

Yes, I still need the faith to heal, but I know I already walk in the "compassion and love" that God will use. God has answers for this world's sicknesses and the Cross and the stripes of Jesus purchased our right to be healed. Lack of faith and lack of knowledge in the area of healing is keeping many people sick.

I know that if Jesus tells me to pray for people, that He is going to do something.

Heavenly Father,

Teach us Your ways and the ways Your Son. Increase our compassion for others. Stir up in us the passion and the faith to heal. In Jesus' name, I ask. Amen.

Kingdom Nugget 38
Being Led By the Holy Spirit

Have you ever seen the game of hop scotch being played? Squares are drawn with chalk on a path or sidewalk and young girls hop though them in an enthusiastic and creative way, two legs together, then hopping on one leg followed by two legs apart and so on. It is really fascinating to see little girls at play in this simple way.

That is how we all should be, Jesus has laid out the chalk markings on the path and all we need to do, to be led by the Holy Spirit, is to follow the commands that He drew in the path for us. Walking in the Holy Spirit is all about being a child and having the childlike faith that Father God, like any good earthly "Papa," knows what is best for His Own precious children.

A young child doesn't bother their daddy with such things like, where money comes from, nor do they ask their daddy how much money is needed to put food on the table. A child is just a child and their thoughts include such things as which toy will they next play with and what video in their collection will they watch next. Children don't seem worried about any of the things that parents worry about.

Walking in the Holy Spirit is being like that. It's being mindful that your Father is always looking out for your good. As an adult, walking in the Holy Spirit is daily enjoying a deep and intimate relationship with Jesus. You have the absolute assurance that both Jesus and the Holy Spirit will continually guide and direct you in all the decisions you make.

Of course, to be led by Jesus or the Holy Spirit, you would first have to be able to hear them speak to your spirit/heart. Once you know the commands of Jesus and you have a heart of love toward men and God, and you can hear from Jesus and the Holy Spirit on decisions that are not covered in the Bible, then you can know that you are indeed walking in the Holy Spirit.

I am trying to make it sound easy, but truly, developing a relationship with God takes effort and time on our part. That's because all great relationships take time to develop. Good relationships take commitment and perseverance. God yearns for personal relationship with all people, but it took me many years to come into my present day relationship with Jesus and the Holy Spirit. It hasn't been easy, because our old sin nature and the devil never stops reminding us of our shortcomings.

Today, a friend of mine said that I reminded her of Jesus. When I had earlier spoken to her on the phone, Jesus was using my voice and was speaking though me, to her. At the time, I really didn't feel that I was prophesying to her, I was simply giving her some advice. However, her spiritual ears discerned that Jesus was using me to have this heart to heart conversation with her. She said that despite the fact that she had paused many times during the conversation, she wasn't being rude, but rather, she had been overwhelmed by what Jesus had said to her.

I was astonished that Jesus would speak through me without me being aware of it! Also today, I prophesied to a friend and I thought Jesus was speaking to him through me. My friend said that it took him a while to work out what was happening. He told me that it wasn't only Jesus speaking to him but the whole three persons of the trinity were speaking to him. I asked him why he thought that. He said that I was using the plural word "we" instead of the single word "I". I was being used by God in a new way, yet I had no idea of it at the time.

Being led by the Holy Spirit is when He is using your body, mind and spirit to do God's will. This will happen when you put your own flesh in the back seat and the Holy Spirit is given full reign in your life.

The flesh will always war against the Spirit. At times, what the Spirit wants to do through you may seem crazy to your natural mind. For example, it doesn't make sense to turn the other cheek when you have been offended. Your fleshly mind wants you to tell the pastor that someone has greatly offended you, so that the offender can be chastised. Forgiving him, loving him, turning the other cheek and praying for him simply sounds ludicrous to our old mindset, but that is what Jesus taught us to do in His commands.

Heavenly Father,

Show the reader Your ways. Lead them to Your Son's commands in the Bible and give them the grace to begin to walk in them. If they are not hearing Jesus and the Holy Spirit speak to their spirit, please bring to their remembrance the time they purposely ignored such a prompting and give them the grace to be able to reconnect, so as to fix this blockage. In Jesus' name, I ask. Amen.

Kingdom Nugget 39
Finding Purpose and Living In It

I was thirty years old when I read a life changing book on purpose and personality and how that plays out in our life. This book was one of the top five books I have ever read and it not only impacted me, but it changed me. I simply found myself as I discovered who I was created to be, what my personality type was and what sort of work would give me the most satisfaction.

My personality was described as being a person who was most happy steering people toward excelling in their gifts and talents. I was described as a gifted communicator who does very well as a teacher, public speaker or minister. I was so excited to read these things for they just resonated so deeply with me.

I have listed below some of the things that I learnt about my personality:

- "Teachers expect the very best of those around them, and their enthusiasm inspires action in others and the desire to live up to their expectations."

- "In orientation, they are altruistic, credulous, mystical, situated on pathways and with their eye on tomorrow. They base their self image on being seen as empathic, benevolent, and authentic. Often enthusiastic, they trust intuition, yearn for romance, seek identity, prize recognition, and aspire to the wisdom of the sage."

- "These outgoing mentors arrange work and social engagements ahead of time and tend to be absolutely reliable in honoring these commitments."

- "In some teachers, inspired by the responsiveness of their students or followers, this can amount to a kind of genius which other types find hard to emulate."

I am a prophet who has been called to prophesy, preach and teach with words and through writing. I have been told that I come across as a sage and tonight, I downloaded this book and it has the word "sage" mentioned in it. I have been called by God and I am a mystical person also, and so much of what I quoted is true of me.

The first step on a very successful journey with God is to know who you are created to be.

In David Kersley's book," Please Understand Me", which I earlier quoted, I discovered most of the information about what I was created to be. In other research under my personality type, I found a list of occupations that such a person with my personality would be most fulfilled in.

I cannot stress how a good walk with God becomes a reality with knowing what you are here on earth to do. Knowing that I am born to teach keeps this flame within me alive, it keeps me writing and publishing books, and it keeps me posting status updates that I believe will encourage my friends on Facebook.

You can also do a spiritual gifts test on a site found on a Google search and be rated against all the spiritual gifts. Knowing your first six or seven strongest spiritual gifts can point you in the direction of what you need to be doing.

The highest two gifts of mine are the gift of poverty (willing to live on little money so all available money goes to Gods work) and the gift of giving (the gift that supplies the happiness and joy that goes with the gift of poverty.) These gifts have enabled me to publish the books God has led me to write. I have now found a publisher who publishes my books.

Those who couldn't go without life's luxuries and life's so called fun couldn't spend thirty percent of their income each week on God and His purposes. In the past two years since my book on the parables has been published on Amazon, five hundred people have bought it and four thousand and five hundred people have downloaded it for free on Kindle. Do you know if only ten percent of the readers of that book do what I suggest, then five hundred people are living their life differently because of something little old me wrote and published? As a teacher, this gives me great joy and purpose in life.

Two other spiritual gifts of mine are the gift of encouragement and the gift of prophecy.

I have been saved and renewed by the love and grace of God, demonstrated by the life and death of Jesus. Therefore, I wholeheartedly endorse the grace teaching of the New Covenant. Prophecy that I give individuals and churches is very encouraging, so both of these gifts work closely together. I am also very observant and very quick to give a person an edifying word about some character trait they are excelling in, or their appearance or anything that stands out to me as extra special.

After those four prior gifts is the teaching gift that God has entrusted to me.

The reason why I continually stretch myself financially in self-publishing is that I wanted to reach out to as many readers as I can. I was not writing for monetory purposes, far from it. My purpose is to teach Christians a better way to live. That's why I have used Kindle to distribute my books and have some of them free from time to time. God knew my heart when He gave me the gifts that He did.

Do you pick up that I am excited about my life and my future?

Determine to no longer live without direction and life purpose, I strongly suggest that you read David Kersley's book," Please Understand Me." Take the time to do a spiritual gifts test. Also do the Myres Briggs personality type test so you can research more about yourself.

Heavenly Father,

I ask that You will inspire these people who read this chapter to find out for themselves who they are in Christ, and what they were created to do with their life, in order to fill their lives with joy. In Jesus' name, I ask. Amen.

Homework: Describe for all of us what you think your personal purpose in life is.

Kingdom Nugget 40
What Are the Eternal Rewards?

With Heaven being a cashless society, what rewards could there be for people on earth who have given a lot of time and money to the Lord? In what way will the faithful be rewarded?

Jesus said that in His Father's house were many mansions. Therefore, Christians can rightly assume that when they arrive in Heaven, there will be a special mansion waiting for them.

The first time, I had a vision of my home in Heaven, Jesus and I sat on a couple of easy chairs and He served me a drink with pineapple juice and coconut rum. When I was home in bed watching the vision, I heard Jesus say the name of the drink and I had not heard it before, but it put a fresh burst of pineapple into my mouth. Before us was an expanse of water with sail boats sailing on it. My auntie and uncle have lived in two homes with magnificent water views and Jesus must have known that having such a view had always been a desire of mine.

The second time I went to my Heavenly home, I noticed it was three stories high. The inside had beautiful exposed beams which gave it a very rustic feeling. It had polished wooden floors throughout with colorful throw rugs. A beautiful fireplace was in the living room and circular stairs led up to the second level. Running down the inside walls were inbuilt fish tanks with magnificent tropical fish gracefully swimming around. The fish could somehow swim into whatever room you walked into and they basically followed you around the home.

When I was young, my older cousin had a tropical fish tank and I really wished I had one too. Jesus, in His love, had specially incorporated this wonderful feature just for me. In my living room is a very large painting of a lion and a lamb lying down peacefully together and at times, when you look at these animals, they actually come to life! This particular picture also acts as a portal to another place in Heaven where children live.

The third time I visited my home in Heaven, I met my cat that had died when I was eight years old. In my vision, my cat actually spoke to me and even prophesied over me. He told me that my roommate, whom I had just told to vacate my Housing Commission apartment, was going to move out without any fuss. This had been a concern to me, but my faithful cat had reassured me that all would go well. (If a departed "cat" can talk to me in a vision about Heaven, then it seems logical to me that our loved ones in Heaven really do know what is going on in earth.)

A week later, my roommate moved out with no fuss whatsoever. Even better, he has continued to remain a friend and talks to me as if nothing had ever happened between us. This was a very welcome and pleasant surprise to me.

Therefore, I believe that the popular Christian view that animals don't have spirits and souls and thereby will not be in Heaven seems to me to be incorrect. My cat is in Heaven and he has a good recollection of his former life with me, when I was just a young lad.

On one of my Heavenly visits, I also talked to a fish called Harry.

Harry spoke to me and reassured me that my whole future was planned and that I was to relax and take one day at a time. He told me that the Holy Spirit knew just what to tell me each day and how to direct me and so I should not worry about what to do and when to do it, as I will always be told. I was surprised that week to meet a new friend whose name was also Harry. This new friend and I sometimes go out together to do prophetic evangelism on the streets.

My home in Heaven has a center console kitchen and a swimming pool. Both these features were in my much loved auntie and uncle's home as well. My home also has a pier and a cruiser. The boat can sleep eight people and it's very well equipped.

I have shared these things so that you can be certain that you too, will have a lovely home in Heaven, uniquely designed just for you. Jesus has watched you and filled the house and decorated it with all the things that you have loved on earth. If you were extremely poor and lived in Africa in a mud hut, Jesus has your dream home already waiting for you in Heaven.

Jesus knows exactly how to reward me, He brought Mary Magdalene down with Him one time in a vision and she has come to visit me many times since, to be with me on earth. I always wanted to be able to have coffee with her in Heaven as she was one of Jesus' closest friends. I've been told that part of my reward in Heaven is that I will spend a good measure of time with her.

When I am not teaching in Heaven, I am going to serve people in a coffee shop. I will always be spending time with people and having heart to heart chats. I will be the type of shop owner who has staff and is always sitting down with customers and sharing a coffee with them.

My rewards in Heaven will also include:

- The people who have been touched by my books will be known by me in Heaven.

- The people I have given prophetic words to on earth who later became Christians will meet me and remember what I said to them. Many of these people will become very good friends of mine.

- People who I have loved from a distance, who on earth were popular, like Billy Graham and Michael Jackson, I will have the opportunity to meet.

- The people who have been saved as a result of my giving to mission organizations, I will meet and rejoice that my money had a part in their salvation.

- All of my Facebook friends who are saved, I will meet in Heaven.

Therefore, I know that one day, the idea of having only a few friends and being lonely will be something of the past. This is just a small glimpse of Heavenly rewards. They could fill a whole book instead of this short book chapter.

"Eye has not seen nor has the heart conceived what the Lord has prepared for those that love Him." This is what the Scriptures declare about our home in Heaven.

Heavenly Father,

Please help the readers to become "Heavenly-minded" and invest in missions and Your kingdom, where there will be eternal rewards. Help them to seek treasure in Heaven and not earthly lusts. In Jesus' name, I ask this. Amen.

What Rewards In Heaven Are Possible?

God is an extremely creative God! You only have to look at the animal kingdom or the landscapes on earth to know that God is an awesome, creative God.

However, some people on earth will never find their purpose and walk in their destiny. Sadly, not all people learn to hear the voice of God and are directed by Him to their particular destiny. Many people have wonderful dreams on earth and never seem to have the time or the opportunity to carry their dreams out. If you are one of these believers, you can be sure that when you arrive in Heaven, God has great plans for you.

You can be sure if you have never thought about what your perfect job would be, to suit your unique character, that this is not the case with God. God knows what you were originally created for, so when you settle into Heaven, you will discover that you will be doing the very best thing you could think of, as your daily work; it will be a joy and never a chore.

Many people might question me here and say "What is all this talk about work in Heaven? Don't we just praise God all day?"

This common misconception, that we go to the throne room each day and spend the whole time in worship would to me, be somewhat boring. I am delighted therefore, to tell you that there are many things to do in Heaven and it is simply like the earth, but at least a thousand times better. In Heaven, there will be all types of cafes, restaurants, music festivals and bands to see, in fact all sorts of entertainment. There will be the chance to act or sing or be part of a band if that's your desire. There will be plays being performed, movies being made, and professional recording sessions available. If you can dream it, it will be possible for you to do in Heaven.

Not only will you be doing what you were originally designed to do, you will also enjoy wonderful leisure activities. Also, you will have the opportunity to meet with all the Bible saints and converse regularly with them. If you would like to take further studies relating to the character of God or the Bible, you will have the very best teachers to instruct you. Everyone will know each other and it will be an exciting place to be.

Everything you ever did on earth for God and for other people will be rewarded in Heaven. These rewards in Heaven will continue to bring lasting joy. If you provided a free Coca Cola for a homeless man in your city, you will have a favorite drink in Heaven that will never run out. If you provided special delicious meals on earth for strangers, people in Heaven will provide the very same meals for you, with a Heavenly touch of course.

More than you can possibly dream of will be yours!

Heavenly Father,

Lord, I ask that you give Your people some insight into what Heaven is like and what rewards await them. Show them that the treasure they store in Heaven is countless times better than the pleasures that they have on earth. Lord, give the people that read this book, dreams of Heaven that will inspire them on. In Jesus' name, I ask. Amen.

Kingdom Nugget 42
Different Glories In Heaven

Jesus spoke much about rewards in Heaven, especially in His parables. A reward is always something you achieve for doing something well. If a person was rewarded on earth through receiving the praises of others, Jesus said that this person had already received their reward. Therefore, we can be sure that the rewards in Heaven are going to be very different to those on earth. Personally, I know that I would definitely prefer an eternal reward in Heaven to the temporary reward from man.

"If anyone's work which he has built on it endures, he will receive a reward." 1 Corinthians 3:14. Also, we read: *"Behold, I am coming quickly, and My reward is with Me, to give to everyone according to his work." Revelation 22:12*

I have heard from a person who has had many visions of Heaven that Heaven's rewards differ from person to person, because of the various glories, (or levels of brightness) according to what they did on earth. He said that people who achieved great things on earth, like Moses, Abraham and the Apostle Paul, shine with a glory that is far brighter than the glory on others.

Because Heaven is perfect in every way, there's no envy about the different levels of glory. The people with less glory have due respect for those who have more glory than they possess.

This makes perfect sense, because even though every believer is saved by Christ's atonement alone, we each live our Christian life with various degrees of enthusiasm, making each of us a special saved individual. Therefore, we are not all the same in passion and personality in Heaven. Our level of glory will differ most importantly according to our heart motive, as well as our achievements in service to God and man whilst on earth.

This is just a very short message for you to ponder.

Heavenly Father, Please give all my readers the courage and enthusiasm to work for Your Kingdom on earth. In Jesus' name. Amen.

Being Rewarded On Earth for Deeds

You may recall that Jesus warned us not to pray in front of others so they could admire our style of praying, because if we seek and receive the praise of man, then we have already received our reward on earth and will thereby forfeit our Heavenly reward. To remove ourselves from this type of temptation, Jesus suggested for us to isolate ourselves from others, to be alone with God and pray to Him in private and in doing so, we will be rewarded by Him, which to my mind is far better.

I remember when I was only about fourteen years old, I used to go to a Bible study with a group of young Christian surfers. Each week, when it came to prayer time, I made sure my prayer was the most eloquent. Not only that but all the way through the prayer time, the others would hear my spontaneous "yes" and "amen!" When everyone had prayed, people used to pat me on the back and say things like, "Always love to hear you pray, man."

At the time, I thought that I had the reputation as the best prayer in the group. I was so happy in those days and I thought I was so good. Now looking back, I know that all I was doing was feeding my own ego. My eloquent prayers probably didn't go higher than my own head.

About thirteen years ago, I received a tract from some guys called "The Jesus Christians" and they went into the commands of Jesus. One of the commands was not to pray in public and they totally explained that my kind of prayer was the type that God does not approve of. (Being an "off" or "on" sort of a guy, from that time on, I have stopped praying in public.)

When asked to pray in public, I cannot help this old side of me from coming out, so I abstain from public praying. I know there are many mature Christians or even baby Christians who don't feel the need to boost their own ego like I once did. There would be many Spirit led believers who pray with a right heart attitude, but I am just saying, it's something we have to be mindful about. Jesus knew what was in the hearts of men and hypocrisy in any form is not pleasing to God.

Jesus also said that we should not give to the poor or give alms in front of others, so it could be seen, as He said our reward in Heaven would be withdrawn. Therefore, today, if people know of our giving and then give us personal praise for it, do we forfeit our reward in Heaven? It's a point to ponder. Jesus says that our giving should be so personal that even our right hand should not know what our left hand has done. That sounds pretty personal!

You may not be even seeking rewards from Heaven in what you do. You might have a good heart and simply want to pray and to give to others without any reward. If this is the case, do it in private anyway if you can manage it, because the Lord doesn't want His children looking for the praise of man.

Please don't think I'm getting all "religious" here in what I have said. It's quite okay to go to a prayer meeting and keep your prayer free of boasting. It's quite okay to give to a plate being passed around for a missionary. I don't want to sound like I am placing limitations on you. It is just that in all things, we are to check our heart motive. That is the message I'm trying to convey. God will not share His glory with man.

Heavenly Father,

Allow this lesson to sink into the people the way that you want it to and bring about change in their life, if that needs to happen. Thank You for blessing Your people and open up the floodgates of Heaven. In Jesus' name, I ask. Amen.

Doing Things In Private

Jesus encouraged us to do things in private. He said if we do things in private, that we would be rewarded in Heaven for our good deeds. I well know that it doesn't have the same buzz to do something that no one knows about. It's sometimes good to have people know what you have done. It is always fun sharing something, but God knows the human heart and sometimes we would do it more for the praise we receive, than for the simple fact of doing it.

For the sake of sharing, here are some ideas you may be interested in, even though I did these things in private at the time. This is coming from the right heart. I am just trying to give you new ways of blessing others. I really love missions and giving to poor people.

There is an organization you can find on the Internet: it's a site called "Heavens Family." I bought two push bikes for one hundred dollars, for missionaries/evangelists in India. An evangelist with a push bike can ride hundreds of miles to many villages, instead of having to walk vast distances. Buying a bike for this purpose would give you half of the reward of the souls that he saves. I liked the idea of a happy Indian evangelist getting on his push bike and starting off with blanket, tent and clothes to do fulltime mission work. This was a once off gift, the type I like doing when I have the opportunity.

Another time, I felt led to supply a book on the basics of the Christian faith to about ten student pastors. The book has about four hundred pages, so it's very comprehensive. This was also organized through "Heavens Family." The particular male students who received my book were then able to teach great things to their people. The simple Bible Schools that these men attended couldn't afford to pay for the book.

My donation gave me pleasure and the men would have a great resource tool on their book shelf to come back to, time and time again. I gave one to my senior pastor in Australia who did a lot of mission work overseas and he said that he agreed with everything the book taught and asked me where he could order more copies.

One time, I saw Oprah Winfrey had advertised an organization called "Kiva" who gives small business loans to impoverished people overseas. These small loans allow them to start a small business and give them the opportunity to come out of poverty by earning a living for their family. This is called "Micro finance." I originally contributed about three hundred dollars to the organization. As the personal loans are paid back, I lend the money to another person.

One time I was short of money myself, so I took two hundred dollars back, so today I still have one hundred dollars going out on loans from time to time in twenty-five dollar agreements. This is a gift that keeps on giving and Kiva was loved by Oprah so I know she had done her research.

There is an organization called Far East Broadcasting Company (FEBC). They do missions and mostly, they broadcast Christian Radio into regions and countries that don't have many Christians. You can buy a wind-up radio (for places with no power) for a small community to listen to the radio programs. The company claims that on average, thirty lives are touched by this simple method of evangelism with the use of just one donated radio. I have bought a number of these radios for this company's use.

I have the gift of giving therefore this gift makes it a real pleasure to give when the Lord prompts me to. God knows why I have shared about these mission organizations. He knows that my only reason for doing so is to give my reader an opportunity to give to others less fortunate, and not to boast about my own good works. If only one person gives, due to this Kingdom Nugget, it will have been worth it to God.

Don't ever tire of giving in private. It may not be popular to give without people knowing, but there is a reward waiting for you in Heaven right now. God loves you.

Heavenly Father, Please encourage people to give to others, Lord. Touch people's hearts as they read this and give them the desire to give to your mission field. In Jesus' name, I ask. Amen.

Nothing Is Too Small a Gift.

A gift that you give to an organization might just pay a wage for a bookkeeper in that organization. Your gift could be used in advertising for them, or on making their website run, or any number of a hundred things that don't seem spiritually important. You might not think that paying for the running costs of a mission organization is a good thing at all. You might want the money you give to go direct to the front line. Many organizations know this and split their gift giving up, in such a way that this can happen.

I want you to know that no amount of money is too small. I want to reassure you that if you gave one thousand dollars toward having a well dug in Africa, or donated twenty dollars for a book to be bought for a pastor to refer to, each has God's seal of approval. No matter how big your gift, God has angels who make sure the gift has its positive impact. Just changing one life for the better is a good thing.

Once, a close friend of mine gave me just a paragraph out of the book "A Prodigal God" to read. This short reading impacted me so much it started me on the road to change my whole way of believing in Christ. I discovered in that one paragraph that I had been a self righteous "spiritual jerk" to others. This revelation completely shocked me and made me read more.

What if you were the one to buy a book for missions and that book make a dramatic impact in someone. I have written three books since then and throughout these books, there is a grace message, not a legalistic message that I had once been a slave to. What if you had been the person to turn me around?

Satan likes to make us think that we are not important.

The ten dollars you may give each week to your church may just pay for part of the utilities. You may think, "What good is it for me, even giving this money?" You might be right to think that way. But there is a different way of seeing the value of your donation.

What about that lady weeping up the front at the altar call? If they didn't have enough money to pay for the lights to be on, church might not be on, and that lady might not be receiving her breakthrough. In all our church giving, the money is used for God's Kingdom purposes. Therefore, each week, there are people in your church growing in the Lord because of the gift that you give to further God's unique purposes for that spiritual home!

Every cent I earn from my books goes back to producing more books.

Jesus told me last week that I am never going to run out of things to write about. So if you bought this book, your money is going toward another book. What would happen if your money helped make a book that totally turned hundreds of lives around forever? What would that mean to you?

Don't let the enemy steal your joy. Oh yes, he will come up with many things to say to you. He will say that your church isn't saving people and so you shouldn't support it. You should send your money to a TV evangelist who promises to give you a tenfold return on your money. Yes, the devil is crafty and he is only interested in reducing God's Kingdom on earth.

Just sending twenty people you know the link to the Amazon page that this book will be on one day will be a great thing. Posting the book on Facebook would be a great thing. My point is that anything that you do for the Kingdom of God is a good thing.

Just sending twenty dollars towards a well being dug in Africa may pay for one family in the village to get clean water for the rest of their life. Wouldn't you like to know that family? Your gift doesn't have to be big for the Lord to use it.

Heavenly Father,

I would love for Your angels to speak to this reader and encourage them for all the giving that they have done. Fill them Lord, each time they give with good thoughts of encouragement. Have Your guardian angels bless the people that read this and give to you. In Jesus' name, I ask. Amen.

Kingdom Nugget 46
God's Will Versus
Your Own Will

Sometimes, knowing God's personal will for you may seem hard. Even when you speak to Jesus and are led by the Holy Spirit, it isn't always evident that you are doing God's will. God likes to lead us all into His will but He never forces any of us into it.

God has a plan for every life. He knows what is best for each of us, but so many times, we just like to do things on our own. It takes quite a bit of listening and following direction to get onto the path that God has in mind for us.

My life was ruled by sin for many years, I chased after the yearnings of my flesh. It's only in the last couple of years that I have started to walk with God and have begun to write books. I see now that God always wanted me to be a teacher through my books and I am busy now producing them one after another. It takes time, like I said, for some people to be open to receive clear direction about God's perfect will for their life.

It would be far easier if when we were born-again, we received a list of personal instructions and directions from God. Yes, when we were converted, we soon had a Bible, but that takes years to understand. Many of us would find it extremely helpful to know on a piece of paper exactly what they personally were meant to do with their life. I know so many sincere Christians who grapple with this question for many years before finding their life purpose.

The fact that things are not made clear to us means that God wants us to experience the journey of discovering His will and He very much wants to be part of the process. He wants us to discover what makes us tick and He wants us to find something that we enjoy that brings Him glory. He then wants us to pursue that particular thing with all our heart.

I am so happy and thankful, that I have found God's purpose for my life and I will pray that all my readers will discover their particular role in life as well.

Heavenly Father,

I ask that You lead the reader to discover for themselves, Your specific will for them. Show them bit by bit, what Your will looks like and lead them into doing it. Use other people, even prophets, and speak to the person direct until they know what You want them to do. In Jesus' name, I ask Amen.

Are We Really Sheep?

"Come, you blessed of My Father, inherit the kingdom prepared for you from the foundation of the world; for I was hungry and you gave Me food; I was thirsty and you gave Me drink; I was a stranger and you took Me in; I was naked and you clothed Me; I was sick and you visited Me; I was in prison and you came to Me."

"Then the righteous will answer Him, saying, 'Lord, when did we see You hungry and feed You, or thirsty and give You drink? When did we see You a stranger and take You in, or naked and clothe You? Or when did we see You sick, or in prison, and come to You? And the King will answer and say to them, 'Assuredly, I say to you, inasmuch as you did it to one of the least of these, My brethren, you did it to Me." Matthew 25:34b-40

We are all familiar with the parable of the sheep and the goats, so I may not bring anything new to you. I look at this parable as both a warning and an encouragement to have a good look at ourselves and our everyday conduct in our Christian life.

When was the last time you came across a person who was thirsty and you gave them a drink? Of course, this is not just limited to a physical drink. This could refer also to a person who is hungry for spiritual life giving water and you could supply it to them by sharing the Gospel so that they could have the Living Water inside of them. When is the last time either of these events happened to you?

A good friend of mine says that this parable is not for Christians. However, the quote in the second paragraph refers to the righteous, so Jesus is talking to Christians. However, I know that quite a few of God's sheep do not treat others as they would treat the Lord Jesus Christ.

Jesus told this parable for a good reason. Many people simply do not make a habit of hanging around people who are hungry, thirsty and naked. These people are always in your city if you care to look for them. Many of these people are always begging for money on the streets. Buying a beggar just a hot or a cold drink is a gift that such a person could not repay. I think Jesus wants us to open our eyes to the need that is out there in every community.

Jesus is aware of your heart. He knows you and what you are made of. He knows all about you. I think it's time to reflect on this passage and be aware that how we act in this way is a practical way of building your reward in Heaven and pleasing the Father while on earth.

Heavenly Father,

Open our eyes to the opportunities to serve the hurting and the broken. Open our hearts to the people who could do with help and lead us to give of ourselves in this way. In Jesus' name, I ask. Amen.

Bringing Love and Grace to the World

Is the world that you live in a better place because you are in it? When you are not around for a while, are people happy to see you when you return? Do people tell you that you mean a lot to them? You might not be a part of a great community like I am, so the answer to these questions might be "No!" If that's the case, it doesn't mean you are not a great person.

It's important not to just know about the subject of God's grace, but to also be a dispenser of His grace to others. In other words, it's vital that we don't just know grace in theory because God's grace is something that we constantly need to pass on to others.

On Facebook, I have a number of people as friends that preach God's incredible grace. Some of them are really passionate about the subject. I made a post once that one of them didn't agree with and he became very rude to me. I told him that his behavior was rude and he became even ruder. I asked him to please excuse my post if it offended him that much and he kept posting other rude remarks. My point for sharing this is that we need to move in grace and love all the time, not just preach about it.

I have found some grace preachers on Facebook who are really quick to condemn people and label them as being a legalist or religious, and yet, if they had more grace, they would not be so fast to condemn others who have not yet seen the light. I know this only too well as I too have been guilty of this in past.

One way to learn about grace is through Christian books. One book that immediately comes to mind is "Extraordinary Grace" by John Bevere. We learn about grace through people who constantly exhibit it in all situations and with all people. On a personal level, we are aware of God's underserved grace whenever we ask forgiveness.

I have found that having "grace" people in my life is a wonderful way to learn what grace looks like. It is through the example of others that you too can learn to walk in grace. Being forgiven so much by Jesus is also a powerful example of God's awesome love and grace.

It is important as I have said, not just to know about love and grace, but to live it out in our lives. Loving the unlovely, bearing with "the annoying" people, and forgiving those that strike us in some way, are all ways we can bring the Lord honor and glory in our lives.

Many non-Christians, who know we are believers, like to test our ability to love. They want to know and experience an authentic love. It is these kinds of tests that we need to pass, so the Holy Spirit can convict the heart of those who test us.

Love does conquer all! Nothing can withstand the power of God's love. In this life, we all have a calling to be ambassadors of the Lord Jesus Christ to the world. As Christians, we should all be "little Christs" to others. Sure, there will be times when we really blow it and there will be times when we only just miss the mark! But we can still ask a person for forgiveness when we mess up. It makes a great statement when a Christian asks a non-Christian for forgiveness.

We need to walk in humility, so when we do mess up, we have the courage to go and do some repair work. One day in glory, I will be perfect, but until then, I will probably have quite a few messes to clean up and repair. However, I do love differently these days and I do show grace to others differently these days, and through most of my behavior, I am storing up treasure in Heaven.

Heavenly Father,

Teach us what true love and grace are. Show us through books, through people, and through Your love of us when we mess up. Teach us to walk in more love and grace for others from this day on. In Jesus' name, I ask. Amen.

Kingdom Nugget 49
Big Ministry or Normal

Are we all called to a big ministry? Most people would respond with "No!" Surely, the ministry of Joyce Meyer, Joseph Prince and Andrew Wommack are big ministries. These are all ministries I follow and all of them have TV Shows around the world. But what is a big ministry and what is important to God?

Do you know that if you've been used by the Holy Spirit to bring someone to salvation, then that was a really important work! Not only here on earth was much rejoicing, but the angels in Heaven rejoiced as well.

For those believers who have not yet personally led someone to Jesus, I want to stress that just being "God's light" in this dark world is an extremely important ministry. This is because you would be unknowingly sowing Kingdom seed into the lives of many people, perhaps for someone later on to do the work of harvest.

God needs us little people. He needs people to be themselves and if being a normal, on fire Christian is what He wants of you, than that is what you will be. There are so many people watching us in this sin sick world. Many of these onlookers live their life without hope and purpose and they are watching closely how a believer in Jesus copes with life.

As believers, we all want to reach people for Jesus. There are many wonderful books that you can buy and give to those you are praying for. There is a book that women particularly would like, called "Redeeming Love" which would be a very powerful witness to give to a lady who is not yet saved. For people who enjoy suspense, there is a book called "Beyond Justice" by Joshua

Graham which is a great witnessing tool. Both novels are very powerful and if you want to witness to someone who loves reading, they are also great books to give to a non-Christian.

Are you good at prayer? Do you like to pray? Do you often receive answers to your prayers? You could influence a big ministry by becoming an intercessor for them. Sure, you may be a little person, but God would use your prayers to influence the nations. My life is a whole lot better since people have started to pray for me. I know just how great prayer is. Do you realize that your prayers could achieve mighty things for God and His Kingdom's purpose?

Are you a gifted business person? Do you earn good money? Perhaps your business product or service could help other people in ministry and because you are in business, you could do work for them cheaper than anyone else or even perhaps for free.

There are hundreds of ways to be used. Many people feel that they are not good at anything and therefore, God won't use them. As I have said, the two books I mentioned are an easy way of reaching out to people. I have personally found this to be true.

I want to impress on you that God doesn't want you to ever consider that you would be of little use to God's Kingdom purposes. If God wanted you to be a "big" person in ministry, He would have told you that one day, you are going to be mightily used by Him. If He has not told you this, try and do something with the position that you currently hold. I am just a little person, but God has given me a desire to write books. I'm no one great, but God is using me. Therefore, He can certainly use you.

Heavenly Father,

Give the reader peace and revelation about who they are in You!

Give them assurance of Your total love and acceptance and give them the opportunity to impact their friends and community with Your love and grace. In Jesus' name, I ask. Amen.

Being Who You Were Destined to Be

I was created to write, to teach, to encourage and to prophesy. I was born to smile and to let people know that God is real and He speaks to me. I am gifted in a number of ways and through a tumultuous battle with sin, with life in general, and with mental illness, my life now serves to bring God glory in all I do and say. However, it hasn't always been that way. God has been so good to me and I am particularly grateful for His wonderful gifts:

- It's a real gift from God to be able to speak to anyone that God wants me to, with a personalized message from Him.

- It's a real gift from God to be able to experience visions of Heaven and share them with people.

- It's a real gift from God to be open to new information by other writers or speakers, to then process it and then be able to teach what I have discovered either by these natural means or by direct revelation from God.

I am eternally thankful that I am able to type and to write and that God has led me to a great publisher. Walking in my calling brings me tremendous joy and when you are living the life that you were destined to live, you too, will experience that same joy.

The fact that I have overcome the constraints of mental illness and the despair of teenage sexual abuse has resulted in me giving inspiration to those who know my story. Also, having had thirty two years addicted to pornography and then conquering that demon of lust is encouraging news to those who are still addicted and who live with constant regret and guilt.

My life and my story is truly a testament to the grace of God.

More of my life's journey can be found in my book "His Redeeming Love" which is soon to be published. (This book is not for the innocent or fainthearted, as I have purposely been extremely blunt and honest.) Sharing my life of pain and my exploits with God will hopefully encourage many people into confessing their own struggle with sin and in doing so, a breakthough will be on its way. I can personally testify that sin loses its power when brought into the light. In my case, this has been definitely true and God's Word confirms it.

"He who covers his sins will not prosper, but whoever confesses and forsakes them will have mercy." Proverbs 28:13

The devil loves for us to live in shame, because he loves darkness and hates the light. By recording my own testimony in "His Redeeming Love," I have personally proved once and for all that the way to break Satan's devastating stronghold is to bring things out in the open so it cannot be hidden anymore. The book has been healing to me personally and hopefully, others may find the same release and victory that I have now found.

God has given special abilities and talents to every single person ever born. It's hard sometimes to personally recognize these things but those who know you well can help you discover your gifts. Once your purpose for life is found and pursued, there is nothing that compares to it. You don't even have to be a Christian to find your life's purpose, but find it you must. It's not until you have found it that life will have its best meaning for you. When you are aware of your purpose and are living in it, it's extremely rewarding.

Today, being June 2013, I am forty six years old. It has taken me a long time before I came to this understanding about my life, but now that I have been successful "in finding" myself, I plan to busy myself doing what I was originally created to do. I rejoice that I have found both my purpose and passion and I am very grateful for all the goodness of God in my life.

Heavenly Father,

I pray that the reader will seek Your face and discover their ordained purpose in life. I pray that when they find this out, that You give to them the confidence, joy and enthusiasm to walk in their purpose. I ask this in Jesus' name. Amen.

Kingdom Nugget 51
Giving to God

Like me, many believers are sick and tired of messages about giving their money to God. Some churches have a mini sermon every week, before the offering is taken up, to encourage (or guilt trip) the congregation   into giving and yet, in some of these churches, the offering ushers take the plate down the aisle and it mostly has coins dropped into it.

I want to emphatically stress that God looks at your heart. But also know that, yes, He dearly loves a generous giver. Why? An apostle once told me that a believer's wallet is the very last thing to be "converted." Giving to God therefore, is an act of faith in the goodness of God, just like salvation itself.

A husband doesn't go to work for forty years to pay off a house simply because he adores his job. Most husbands go to work, day in and day out, because they love their wife and family. Therefore, they do all they can do to provide for them. In these hard times, just getting bills paid, putting food on the table and providing decent clothes to wear, seems to take all the money earned and then some. The last thing that husband needs is to hear every week, when they go to church, that God will bless them a hundredfold if they give their money to Him every week.

"Like how?" he silently asks himself. Is God going to increase my salary by tenfold or a hundredfold? Therefore, just how exactly is God going to give him a tenfold return on a ten percent tithe? That's like God doubling your income if you give Him ten percent. Many husbands don't fall for the crafty prosperity Gospel - well not all the time and not for long.

You might be surprised that when you get involved in giving to God, by contributing to things that you are excited about, that you can manage to even give up to thirty percent of your income. I am on a disability pension yet I give so much to the Lord that it seems impossible even for me, to reason out God's miraculous accounting skills. I have a sister and two brothers yet dad's wage was very low, but my Christian parents have proved time and time again that it is absolutely impossible to outgive God. He will simply not allow us to outgive Him. That's why in Malachi 3:10, God Himself challenges us to test Him regarding finances.

I have personally found that one of the keys to giving is finding something, or some ministry that you can get passionate about and then support it. These days, most of my money goes on preparing my books. Only ten percent of people that receive my books buy them. Ninety percent of the people reading my books have downloaded them for free on Kindle. I get very excited every time I can give some of my books away on Kindle for five days out of every ninety days. Why? This is because heaps more people will read them and hopefully grow in the Lord!

I also give to three other ministries that I love. Two of these ministries I have already spoken about in a previous nugget but the third ministry I give to is to a grace ministry called Revival or Riots. All of these groups do great work and I give money to them, not on a regular basis, but from time to time.

Remember, Jesus looks only at your heart. Therefore, He wants you to give what you are happy to give. You need not feel condemned. Go and check out those names I mentioned and see if you can get excited. Perhaps, if you feel led to do so, you can even give my books away to your friends as gifts.

Heavenly Father,

Heal the wounded hearts of those who read this. Much damage has been done around this subject. Minister to these people and rebuild their hope that there are good ministries out there to support with their money. In Jesus' name, I ask, Amen.

Kingdom Nugget 52
Prayer and Intercession

Practical reward building prayer and intercession is certainly one of God's Kingdom nuggets that must rate a mention. So many things of earth would not happen if it were not for the prayers of the saints.

I personally believe that every Christian has been brought into God's Kingdom by the faithful prayers of someone close to them. Of course, salvation could just happen because God planned it that way, but I have found that most people who are saved can always tell me about a faithful relative or friend who had been praying for them for years.

I'm a bit of an odd Christian - I only normally pray when I am interceding or praying for another person. I never pray for myself. Jesus and I, or the Father and I just chat with one another. I continually ask questions and I am told the answers. I talk to God and Jesus like I would chat to a person over coffee. It's always a two way conversation and it can go on for quite a while. Not only do I do this before sleeping at night, but often throughout the day, I will have something to say to Jesus, or He has something to say to me. This constant communion throughout the day is what people call praying without ceasing.

Oh, how I wish all people could experience the type of relationship I have with Jesus. If you have trouble hearing God speak to you, ask Him a question and whatever comes into your spirit is His reply. God wants to speak to you, so He's not going to make it difficult. Like everything else in the Christian life, it's our faith in God's total goodness that makes all things work for good.

Some people are called to pray as a vocation or ministry calling. These people receive burdens for others and they actually feel God's emotion about the person and they go into spiritual battle on behalf of the one they are praying for. They continue to do so, until they "feel" in their heart a spiritual breakthrough. These people are very valuable people to the body of Christ and every minister of the Gospel needs these faithful warriors holding them up in prayer. Intercessory prayer is very effective and most of the times, it is truly Spirit led. If you are open and you want to pray for others, I would encourage you to ask God for this gift.

Heavenly Father,

I thank You for blessing Your people and I pray that You will give them the desire to talk to you in a personal and intimate way. In Jesus' name, I ask. Amen.

Kingdom Nugget 53
Jesus... No Condemnation

It is interesting to compare Jesus to the people who are called by His name.

Many believers today are quick to condemn a lady for attending church each week, whilst living with a partner who is not her husband. They feel it's their duty to tell her that her life is not aligned with God's will and yet, when Jesus met a lady living with her partner rather than being married to him, that woman at the well of Samaria was not only "not condemned" by Jesus, but ran and advertised Jesus to all her town folk. She became the first evangelist in the New Testament.

Jesus went on and saved the whole town through the witness of one sinner. What a wonderful testimony to the love and grace of our Savior?

We would probably be all aware of the story when the Pharisees brought a woman caught in adultery to Jesus. The Law of Moses called for death by stoning for such a crime. The Pharisees were ready to do that but first, they wanted to check out what Jesus would do. How would he punish her? What was this radical Rabbi's interpretation of the Law of Moses?

I have heard this preached so often, but have you ever stopped to wonder why this event took place? We know the Bible says that the leaders were trying to catch Jesus out for breaking the Law of Moses, but why did they feel that He would break the Law? Was it that Jesus already had a reputation for displaying a "no condemnation attitude" with the way He treated sinners? Did Jesus have a big resume filled up totally with acts of mercy?

At another time, some particular men brought their crippled friend to Jesus. Such was the crowd that surrounded Jesus that this man was lowered down through the roof on a stretcher, so that he could receive the attention of Rabbi Jesus, the Healer.

Being a cripple, this man was a rejected person in the eyes of the common people. The understanding was that if you were deformed in some way, you or your parents were great sinners. Therefore, this man was used to rejection all of his life. This dramatic determination would have greatly disturbed the household and the crowds of people gathered within.

The crippled man and his friends were obviously desperate to gain the attention of the most Holy Rabbi Jesus! When Jesus gently addressed him as "Son" as He spoke to him, surely the acceptance of the Rabbi in that address, healed a little of that man's heart right away.

Surprisingly, Jesus than went on to say, "your sins are forgiven." Understandingly, the religious hearers of this proclamation instantly murmured that only God could forgive sins. Something to ponder: Have you ever wondered how Jesus could forgive sins when He hadn't yet died for the remission of sins?

This same Jesus who walked the streets of Israel and other places over two thousand years ago still exists today. He is still full of compassion, mercy and patience. These particular qualities about Jesus constantly amaze me. Year after year, He loves me no matter how often I sin. He is still not condemning me but rather, He still reaches out with His hand to pick me up when I sin. He is absolutely incredible! Do you know this same Jesus whom I speak of?

Heavenly Father,

I ask that You show the reader the true character of the Lord Jesus Christ. He is the same, yesterday, today and forever. He loves the sinner; He died for them; He brings no condemnation, but reaches out to bring sinners to Himself. He has never changed! Father, I ask that You give each reader more revelation on what sort of Savior our Lord Jesus really is. In Jesus' name, I ask. Amen.

Kingdom Nugget 54
Jesus... Being Led By the Holy Spirit

In the very first chapter of the Gospel of Mark, we read that Jesus was baptized by John the Baptist and was then immediately "driven" by the Holy Spirit into the wilderness for forty days. This wilderness experience is more detailed in the Gospel of Matthew and Luke.

You would think that once Jesus was publicly baptized in water, that He would have been ready for ministry. But no, Jesus was immediately driven by the Holy Spirit into a wilderness with wild beasts to contend with and nothing to eat for forty long days and nights. Even worse, during this time of physical and emotional weakness, He was tempted by the devil and had to overcome him by the strength of the indwelling Holy Spirit.

We are told in Matthew 4:11, *"Then the devil left Him, and behold, angels came and ministered to Him."*

Fasting, I believe, opens one up to the supernatural in an extraordinary way. In Luke 4:14, it says: *"Then Jesus returned in the power of the Holy Spirit."*

Even in His weakened state, He had put Satan in his place and was now ready to commence His public ministry. If Jesus, the Son of God, needed the power of the Holy Spirit in order to minister to others, so does every believer today.

I surmise that as Jesus reached perhaps His thirtieth day of fasting, He would have been having some pretty awesome visions and conversations with His Father about His future ministry.

Perhaps during that time, in His mind, He may have seen His whole ministry in snap shots. It makes sense to me that He received many supernatural downloads in that time.

It is worth pointing out that as soon as He finished His fast and His time of communion with God, Satan comes to dethrone Him. That is so typical of the enemy. It is true in my life that just prior to a major spiritual breakthrough, all Hell seems to break loose. Sometimes, the intensity of the attack before or shortly after a particular breakthrough actually proves to me the spiritual reality of my breakthrough.

From those first forty days of visions and communion with God, Jesus began to walk in the power of the Holy Spirit by being imbued with the power and direction of the Holy Spirit. Many believers have come and gone since Jesus, and though they have accomplished many great exploits for God through signs and wonders, I am confident that no one has ever been submitted to the Holy Spirit as much as Jesus was when He ministered for three short years.

I read once that Jesus was never interrupted by anyone. He was always doing what the Father wanted Him to do and therefore, every interruption was something God had already seen beforehand and planned for His Son to address. Wouldn't it be so good if we could live a life like that, where every interruption of ours could be a time we take out to minister to that person's need? I know when I am busy and someone I don't know messages me on Facebook, I too easily tell them that I'm busy at the moment, without even dialoguing with them.

To be open to having our days ordered and led by the Holy Spirit like Jesus was would be a precious place to be. I'm sure life would be a lot less worrying in that awesome state. I know being led by the Holy Spirit brings me peace. Knowing I am doing all the Holy Spirit has called me to do is very rewarding and peaceful. I yearn to be a lot more like Jesus in this way. I yearn to be fully submitted to the Holy Spirit and being led in all that I do.

Heavenly Father,

Teach us to hear the Holy Spirit more and more and also lead us to obey His prompting in our lives. Lead us into submission, so that it is natural for us to be led each day by You. In Jesus' name I ask this. Amen.

Jesus... Dependence On His Father

I am not sure in all the preaching I have listened to, that I have often heard how sold out to His Father, Jesus really was. Nor have I often heard people share how much Jesus depended on His Father. When you consider that even His closest disciples didn't realize that their Master's destiny was to die for the whole world's combined sin, you have to wonder how many other things they didn't understand about the Master.

Having had a miraculous conception, Jesus was a man without sin. But even being in that sinless state, it must have caused Him some grief, for He was not like any man that had ever lived, except Adam of course, who was also created sinless. However, Adam later "chose" to sin, but Jesus, though He could have chosen, resisted every temptation known to man.

Jesus on earth had the whole of Heaven watching Him. Even the created angels didn't understand the mystery of Jesus. They were probably saying to each other - why would God the Father send His Son into such a wretched place as planet earth?

Because of His personal revelation of the Scriptures, Jesus was very much alone and with that aloneness, the only One He had full confidence to confide in was with His Father in Heaven.

Some preachers wrongly say that Jesus didn't make a habit of praying, because it's only mentioned a few times in the Gospels that Jesus was up early in the morning to pray. I believe that someone who makes that sort of comment should get to know Jesus well enough to speak to Him. They would soon discover that

Jesus was in prayer by Himself and sometimes with others, nearly every single morning for hours at a time.

Unlike many Christians today, Jesus didn't just pray to God in a one way conversation. He spoke to His Father and His Father spoke back to Him. Prayer is communing with God: it's a two way conversation. His Father would also have shown Jesus visions of each coming day and some of the things He would be doing or confronting. Therefore, in this way, Jesus only did what He saw His Father doing! I believe that Jesus would have had prophetic dreams when He slept and in the morning, with the help of the Holy Spirit, He would receive interpretation of His dreams.

Jesus on earth willingly chose to put Himself under submission to His Father's will. In fact, because of this, many cults have not understood that Jesus was fully God. It was essential for Him to fully identify with man in every way, because God has made His Son to be Judge of the whole earth. In order to do this task, Jesus had to personally understand the battles mankind has to face. Jesus was therefore childlike, in that He didn't promote Himself.

As a human, Jesus was only led by the Holy Spirit. Therefore, He didn't immediately offer to turn the water into wine at a friend's wedding. Instead, He waited for the leading of the Holy Spirit to prompt Him into action. This was His first recorded miracle. I feel that the Holy Spirit might have touched His mother first to gently usher Her Son into the miraculous. I am sure that Mary was not, as many people suggest, overstepping her motherly role.

Jesus had an extremely rich relationship with His Father. He spoke with Him in the early hours of the morning and kept in communion with Him throughout every day. He would have seen visions His Father had given Him come into reality. If He didn't have His Father to dialogue with, Jesus would have had a far more difficult time on earth.

Many of us who have had a bad relationship with our earthly father may struggle to have a deep relationship with our Heavenly Father, but Jesus knows all about that and He wants to heal us in this area so we can love Father God in the way that He deserves to be loved.

Heavenly Father,

Draw us closer and closer to Yourself every day. In Jesus' name, I ask this. Amen.

Jesus... Child Like Faith

What type of person has the faith to bless a few fish and five loaves of bread and then feeds five thousand men, plus women and children? What kind of faith would you need to do such a thing? What sort of faith would allow someone to walk across a lake to help some friends battle against a strong head wind?

Why did Jesus say to us that unless we have faith as a child, that we can by no means enter Heaven? Was being "innocent as a child" the hallmark of Jesus and the key to His powerful ministry?

Many people operating in the prophetic have said to me that I have childlike faith. I think I'm just pretty innocent about some things. I once asked Jesus why I don't see demons when I see angels all around the place. It takes childlike faith to ask a question like that. Jesus told me that if I saw the demons around me, I would never get to sleep at night. I have often pondered why I don't have the part of the discerning of spirits gift that can tell what sort of demon is in a person. I have concluded that I would treat people different if I knew they had a demon.

Jesus was "all knowing" because the Holy Spirit gave Him knowledge. I don't subscribe to the idea that Jesus knew everything that there was to know whilst on earth. If Jesus was not just a normal Spirit-filled believer, how then are we expected to follow in His footsteps and as the Scriptures say: do even greater things than Him?

Jesus relied fully on His Father and the Holy Spirit. He did not move in His own knowledge, but He moved in Godly wisdom. He was not a 'know it all" but spoke to people and allowed them to share things with Him rather than supernaturally know what they were going to tell Him. He could have done a wonderful job of teaching with His revelation of Scripture, but He chose to "hide" many of His teachings in parables, so the truly hungry would search out the nugget of truth within them.

He was grown up, yet He had child-like faith and that is what He wants us to have. That is one reason the children flocked to Him and the animals loved Him. He was not a learned scholar who boasted with His knowledge, but He was a King in beggar's clothes. He was so humble that He didn't even explain to people who He really was, not that they could have handled the revelation anyway. Belief in the true identity of Jesus can only come by faith – that's why His famous parables still remain a mystery to people today.

Yes, He was the Christ, the Anointed One, and yet He lived simply on the favor and giving of the people. He put Himself last, yet He was the first to rise in the morning and the last to lie his head down at night. He walked blindly by faith and was totally led by the Holy Spirit. The attitude He possessed can only be tapped into through humility and child-like faith.

Heavenly Father,

Teach us to live through our Spirit-filled heart and not by human head knowledge. Teach us to be more childlike and rely more on the Holy Spirit's promptings than the dictates of our mind. In Jesus' name, I ask. Amen.

Jesus... Lonely In This World

Many people will come to this nugget and shake their heads. Jesus was lonely in this world? Surely not!

There is a place where you can have so much revelation that you are lonely for others to share that revelation with. There is a place where you can be so full of compassion that you feel your very heart will burst with love and yet when you can't find others that feel the same, you can be very lonely. Jesus would have wept often for the lost sheep of Israel who didn't know His Father like He knew Him. He must have also shed many tears for sick people who didn't come to Him for healing.

Jesus was simply not understood! He brought a new way of thinking about the Law. His message of grace was so foreign to the leaders of the day that at times, they even tried to trick Him into having to choose between law and grace. His actual body was the very New Covenant and He knew when he died and rose again, that all things would be done, but until that had been accomplished, He must have felt that He had only half done His work each day.

The New Covenant or the New Testament has now been around for over two thousand years and yet many churches are not preaching the grace message, but instead preach a mixture of law and grace.

How would it have been for Jesus back then in His day, His very life continually expressing grace and His very body to become God's Perfect Sacrifice for sin for all time? How sad would it have been for Jesus to see the people He came to save, not understanding the very basic rudiments of His message? His closest followers couldn't grasp the fact that He was going to die and rise again on the third day.

We may look at them and say they were quite strange and yet if we were them, we would not have understood either. I really believe that all the information that Jesus knew, but could not share, would have made him very lonely. Sure, He walked with the joy of the Holy Spirit when He was with people, but when alone in the early morning with His Father, the tears would have flowed. Each day would have brought another burden which He had to overcome, by the help of the Holy Spirit's presence and power within Him.

Have you ever read a book that totally transformed your life and then you tried to encourage others to read it, only to find that they were not interested? Well, if you multiplied that sad feeling by thousands, it just may resemble the disappointment Jesus felt each day. Isaiah the Old Testament prophet of God, lived about 690 years before Christ, yet he was divinely led to write that God's future Servant would be a Man of sorrows and acquainted with grief. In fact, the whole of Isaiah Chapter 53 speaks of our suffering Redeemer, the Lord Jesus Christ.

To be our perfect High Priest, Christ Jesus had to know our sorrows by experience. He had to defeat the power of the enemy once and for all. Jesus was a Man on a reconciliation mission so man and God could enjoy fellowship together as was the case in the Garden of Eden. Part of that mission, was the awareness that the Holy Spirit would continue His work in exposing sin and leading us into spiritual truth and power.

Heavenly Father,

Give the reader revelation into the real Jesus that walked this earth, I pray. In Jesus' name, I ask. Amen.

Kingdom Nugget 58
Jesus... The Supernatural

Jesus was not just a normal man with a new style of teaching and a new subject matter. He was not just introducing foreign subjects like, "Love your enemies and pray for those that spitefully use you." But He was underscoring His authority to teach by healing every person who was brought to Him by faith in His ability to heal them.

There exist today some great men of God who are used to heal these days, and yet. the best of them only seem to be able to heal about twenty percent of the people who come before them. Jesus was somewhat more pure and childlike. He simply had the compassion and anointing to heal every single person who came to Him.

He also had the amazing ability to quietly disappear in a crowd when His life was in danger. When they wanted to throw Him off a cliff, or people wanted to seize Him, He was able to disappear into thin air. When a storm wanted to break a boat open and sink it, He was able to talk with authority to the wind, the storm and the sea: "Peace! Be still!" Both the wind and the raging water immediately stilled. When He wanted to cross to the other side of a lake, He was able to walk on water. When five thousand men and their families were hungry, He was able to feed them through a miracle of multiplication.

When presented with a person blind since birth, He opened their eyes and they could see for the first time in their life. When presented with a possessed person who was both deaf and dumb,

Jesus was able to cast the demon out. When presented with a man with thousands of demons, He cast them all out with one command, "Go!"

No, this Jesus was not just a Man of mere words. He had authority over everything it seemed. And these are just a few of the things He said and did. The last verse in the Gospel of John says: *"There are also many other things that Jesus did which if they were written one by one, I suppose that even the world itself could not contain the books that would be written."*

Jesus did a whole lot more and said a whole lot more than what we see in the four Gospels and Jesus is still doing signs and wonders through His servants today.

Heavenly Father,

Bring us all to a place where we would have compassion for the sick and be used to heal a person through prayer. In Jesus' name, I ask. Amen.

Jesus... His True Identity

It is really sad that many Christians grow up with no real idea of their true identity in Jesus. Sure, we are told that we are seated in Heavenly places with Jesus, but few of us live our lives from that position. This was certainly not true of Jesus on earth.

I believe from the age of eight, Jesus knew He was the Messiah. I know the more He heard Scriptures read out, the more He recognized the ones that were about Him. I know from at least the age of eight, He was talking to His Father in Heaven. Jesus knew He was not Joseph's natural born son. He knew He was the Son of God. And when He spoke to God, the Father addressed Him as His Son.

Imagine what life must have been like for Him? Imagine living on earth and not ever sinning! In this aspect alone, He would have known that He was different to other people. With such a deep devotion to His Heavenly Father, Jesus must have grown from one revelation to another, from wisdom to more wisdom.

Jesus did not have any hangups about who He was. Sure, people might have rejected Him and accused Him of doing His signs and wonders by the power of Satan or said that He was mad, but Jesus knew He was the Son of God, the Son of Man prophesied, the King of the Jews, and would ultimately be the Savior of all mankind.

Every Christian needs to know that they are sons and daughters of the King of Kings. They need to know their royal heritage and the privileges and responsibilities this honor incurs. I know that when believers come to really know who they are in Christ, then they will be able to make a lasting difference for good in the world.

Heavenly Father,

Show us who we really are in this world. Lead us to the comforting and victorious knowledge of not only knowing our true identity in Christ but cause us to live and act in that knowledge, every day. In Jesus' name, I ask this. Amen.

Since writing this chapter in 2013, I have written and published a book called "Your Identity in Christ." Look for it on Amazon or soon to be an audio book on Audible.

Kingdom Nugget 60
Jesus... Rejected By Men

Around the time of Jesus, there were a number of people claiming to be the Christ: the Messiah or God's Anointed One. The word "Christ" means the Messiah. The Pharisees had a distorted view of how the long coming Messiah would present Himself, so if anyone claimed this title for themselves, they were tested by a variety of ways to authenticate the true Messiah. This is one of the reasons we see the Pharisees questioning Jesus in the Gospels.

Certain miracles were considered uniquely Messianic in nature. One of them was to cast a demon out of someone who was mute. This miracle in Matthew, Chapter 12 was unique because those who were empowered to carry out exorcisms at that time needed to know the "name" of the particular demon, before they could command it to be gone. Being deaf and dumb, this man was not able to give this information, yet Jesus healed him.

Therefore, when Jesus performed this particular miracle, instead of seeing that He had passed the Messianic Test, the Pharisees hardened their hearts and said that Jesus did this through the power of Beelzebub, which was a term used for the chief of evil spirits. They not only denied God the glory, but had given the glory to the enemy, thereby blaspheming the Holy Spirit. By doing so, the Pharisees had committed the unpardonable sin. (See Matt. 12:31-32)

The Pharisees had been given valid evidence for a Messianic requirement, yet they blatantly refused to admit it and accept Jesus as the One sent by God. Jesus was therefore officially rejected by the powers to be.

However, the sick and the desperate didn't reject Jesus. Also, because of their faith, the publicans and the prostitutes were entering into the Kingdom before the so called righteous.

Sinners openly loved Jesus. His wise and profound teaching seemed to speak to the brokenhearted because they were hungry to learn from Him. Sadly, this was not true of the religious leaders, because they saw Jesus as a threat to their leadership and privileges.

Yet, a day came when Jesus was on trial for treason and the crowds of people loudly shouted that they wanted Barabbas and not Jesus to be released. Amazingly, they now wanted this same Jesus to be crucified! I believe it was this hostile crowd of people, together with the Roman soldiers, that Jesus asked His Father to forgive, "as they knew not what they were doing."

So if you have been rejected, or are still being rejected, Jesus knows how painful that can be. Even to this day, two thousand years later, His people the Jews, largely remain in darkness.

Heavenly Father,

Speak to the hearts of the people who have been rejected and are reading this nugget now. Show them that they are loved and accepted by You and that's all that counts. In Jesus' name, I ask this. Amen.

Jesus... Misunderstood

With all our so called modern knowledge, do we really who Jesus really is? Jesus was and is the King of the whole earth. He is the Son of God who was destined to rule the whole world; only instead of ruling physically, He had to personally, first experience humanity, teach a bunch of disciples and to suffer and die on our behalf.

Yet, His followers didn't have any idea that the coming Messiah was going to suffer. They instead believed that the Messiah would gloriously, forcibly and powerfully take dominion in Jerusalem. He would personally set His people free from being servants to the Romans and to reign as God's anointed King, whom they had long-awaited for.

No one expected a King to come from an obscure town like Nazareth! No one expected the Messiah to be both gentle and mild like Jesus was. Certainly, no one expected the Messiah to lay down His life for sinners! I venture to say that some of the people may have silently hoped that Jesus would miraculously come off the cross. Even at that late stage, perhaps they thought He would take control and set up His kingdom in Jerusalem.

The Pharisees wanted a Messiah just as much, if not more, than the general population, but Jesus was so radical and so different to what they were expecting that they simply could not receive him. The religious leaders prided themselves with having full knowledge of the Scriptures. Jesus therefore, didn't bother to draw their attention to Isaiah 52 and 53 or Psalm 22 to show the people that the Messiah had to suffer death on a cross and then come back years later to set up His Kingdom.

No, Jesus never openly explained that there were two parts to His story, Messiah part 1 and Messiah part 2. Because He didn't explain to the prideful Pharisees these particular Scriptures pertaining to suffering and crucifixion, He was misunderstood by everyone. Even His disciples couldn't understand.

If He wanted to be accepted, if God needed Him to be accepted, He could have proven who He was, but He was born to be misunderstood. He had revelation that would astound the leaders of the Jewish faith, but He chose instead, due to the Holy Spirit's direction, to speak in parables, thereby hiding His wisdom from the prideful. He could have spoken out at His trial, but instead, He was silently spat at, had His beard ripped out, had His back scourged and was hung naked on a cross.

By quoting the first line of Psalm 22, *"My God, My God, why have You forsaken Me,"* He had implied, when it was too late, "look people, this Psalm is being played out now before your eyes." The people who knew the psalm in their hearts saw the prophecy about the crucifixion play out before them. Still, with prophecy being fulfilled, the hardened leaders who wanted Him killed still did not relent or repent.

- Can you imagine being the most powerful man who has ever lived and not have anyone who fully understands who you are?
- Can you grasp how life was to Jesus - to have no one to share His personal information with?
- Can you imagine having the most accurate interpretation of the Scriptures but not being allowed to share them with others?
- Can you imagine being totally obedient to the Holy Spirit and having to continually deny any form of self-centeredness and just for one time be like others?

You see, if you ponder this today, you will agree with me that the Jesus who walked this earth has been grossly misunderstood for over two thousand years. But one day, everyone ever born will face Him!

Heavenly Father,

Show us who Jesus was when he walked this earth and show us who He is now. We do not want to continue with any misunderstanding of Him.

Kingdom Nugget 62

Jesus... Simple, but Profound Wisdom

Many people are familiar with most of the parables. When someone starts reading a parable, we nod for we know what is to come, but few of us know the deep meanings of those simple stories. I looked for years for people to explain them to me. They are just simple stories, but whole books have been written about one particularly: The Prodigal Son. At one stage in my life, God gave me revelation through a lovely friend that I was like the older brother of the prodigal son. Jesus knew that His parables would remain powerful for all time.

Jesus said many hard things: one of His famous teachings was to love our enemies!

This command is simple to hear and pretty easy to understand yet few of us obey it. We pray against our enemies, we pray that unless they repent, they will be struck down and judged by God. We never assume that we could be the problem. Neither do we purpose in our heart to make a conscious decision to love them. Yet, we would gladly acknowledge that Jesus, the Son of God, only gave advice that worked. We openly declare that He was a great Teacher and full of wisdom but we rebel and we do not obey His instructions on how to live a God- glorifying life.

Jesus said not to take your brother in the Lord to court before heathens, as it gives a bad witness of Christ. Yet, so many of us are found in legal disputes and divorce courts today with not one thought that Jesus was also talking about us today, when He spoke this command.

Some people have decided the rules of Jesus are just too hard, so they dismiss them. That type of attitude is actually having Jesus as your Savior but not as your Lord.

Oh yes, Jesus said some things that are easy to understand - simple things. But the wisdom within them is profound. We often don't understand the wisdom of such things as "turn the other cheek" until we have done it a few times and seen for ourselves that it has a good effect on people who have hurt us. It can cause them to question their original opinion and to reach out to us. God is always in favor of reconciliation and He can work in the heart of someone who has hurt us if we do our part according to His ways.

Jesus is not someone you can dismiss or hide from. He is not someone that you can say on Judgment Day, "I really loved You Jesus, but I didn't care for your religious rules."

You see, Jesus didn't come to make our burden on earth harder; He came to give us a better way to live and to behave. He also sent His Holy Spirit to empower us to live His way. He knows what is best for us, and just as His first followers followed Him, so should we.

Heavenly Father,

Give us some insight into just how smart Jesus was on earth and how important His commands are in order to live a victorious Christian life. In Jesus' name, I ask this. Amen.

Jesus Lived for Tomorrow's Reward

Wasn't it Jesus who said we are not to seek the treasures of this world, but we are to focus our attention on our treasures in Heaven? Why would Jesus say such a thing? So what exactly is this treasure that Jesus was talking about?

It says in Hebrews 12:3 that Jesus, for the sake of the joy set before Him, endured the cross. So what is this joy set before Him and what is this eternal treasure in Heaven? US!

We are the joy that was set before Him because we are His treasure. We are his eternal treasure that He had on His mind as they were lashing His back with the flesh-shredding whips. As they hammered the nails into his wrists, we were on His mind. He knew that His death and resurrection story was going to appeal to my heart and to your heart.

You can build treasure in Heaven by giving to the poor, or by supporting a Christian ministry, including your own church. You can gain treasure by supporting people who witness to non-Christians. Whatever you do as a witness for Jesus, whatever noble and godly things you do to lead people to Jesus is potential treasure in Heaven.

The world's treasures only have temporary worth, your brand new smart phone will old technology very quickly and will need replacing, but a refreshing cool drink you may give to a homeless person in your city will be remembered by God for eternity. Your television will fail or need replacing, but that water well you help build in Africa to give people fresh clean drinking water, this will give you eternal reward.

Jesus had His eyes on us at the cross. Jesus knew He was going to win billions of people to Himself when He was despised, rejected, misunderstood and lonely on earth. He knew that one day, He would have millions of friends on earth who He could walk and talk with. Jesus is not lonely anymore. He has some very close friends on earth and in Heaven. He wants us to focus on spending our time and money on eternal things that are not going to be forgotten about, because these things will have eternal and wonderful consequences.

Jesus lived every day fully submitted to the Holy Spirit. He did this as a pattern of how we should live. He lived for eternal rewards – us! Now, His name is above every name on earth and under the earth and in Heaven, both in this age and the one to come. He is now seated at God's right hand, in power and majesty, as He watches people everywhere coming into His Kingdom. Use your time, your abilities and your resources to assist in God's kingdom building program and you will abound in Heavenly treasures.

We are obsessed or worried about so many things but an excellent and simple idea is to develop the habit of asking this question: "In the light of eternity, does my present concern really matter?" You will soon discover that most of the things that we think are important don't really matter at all.

Heavenly Father,

Give us an idea of living for Heaven's rewards. Give us an eternal perspective on life and not just to lust over the things of this world. In Jesus' name, I ask this. Amen.

Kingdom Nugget 64
You Are Spirit, Soul and Flesh

I mentioned this subject in Kingdom Nugget No. 10 but I will go into more detail now.

Most of us are aware that there is more to us than flesh and bones, but many of us don't look very deep into this subject. It's important to know that we are made up of three parts: spirit, soul and body – in that order. Our physical body is only temporary, but our soul and our spirit are eternal – they will live forever, either in Heaven with God or in Hell with demons.

Often, when the Bible talks about the "flesh," it is referring to both our physical body and our unseen and eternal soul area.

Parts of our body are visible, while other parts are hidden. Our physical body has an inner skeleton to support us and organs, blood vessels, sinews, muscles and everything that makes up a healthy human body. Our body needs water, food, rest and sunlight in order to survive. Our body can become tired, hungry or sick if it is not continually maintained correctly. The largest organ in our body is our skin which holds us all together and protects all our inner parts.

Our body's reflection brings us either joy or sorrow. Most of us are too consumed with our appearance and our fleshly appetites, to the point that some of us tend to ignore our important eternal parts, which are our soul and spirit. These are very important to God, because they will live forever.

- Our soul has within it three separate sections:

- Our mind which gives us the capacity to learn and to reason;
- Our emotions or feelings; and most importantly
- Our free-will - this gives us our decision making ability.

It is our will that mostly determines whether we will choose to "believe" or "not to believe" something. Our will therefore determines our actions. Because of this, God will never ever force His will onto our will. Therefore, our will can bring us great grief or enormous delight. This is especially true when we make the awesome choice as to whether we will reject or to accept Jesus as our own personal Savior and Lord.

Therefore, our soul and our spirit makes us uniquely us! Our spirit is sometimes referred to as our heart of hearts. God's Word tell us that, *"The Lord does not see as man sees; for man looks at the outward appearance, but the Lord looks at the heart" I Samuel 16:7*

God looks at our spirit-heart, not our physical organ called our heart.

It is very important to know that at conversion (or salvation), our spirit was instantly made holy and righteous forever, unless of course, if we purposely and defiantly order God to forever get out of our life! Therefore, this is something you would not do unconsciously, or just out of a brief dummy-spit-of-frustration. It would need to be a deliberate choice on your part made by your free will, not just by your emotions.

It's true, our human spirit is perfected the very instant that we ask Jesus to come into our life as Lord and Savior. Our born-again spirit at that instant is therefore innocent and only wants to do the will of God. Know that it is our imperfect soul and our body that begs to disobey God and His ways.

I don't know about you, but when I want to speak to God, as soon as I start drawing close to Him and settle down to pray and listen to Him, my mind takes off with a will of its own! Because of this, I know that my mind is an enemy of all things spiritual. My mind is corrupt and yet, that sadly, is where most people understand their faith from.

We respond to our imperfect soul area, instead of responding to our new born-again spirit. People will use their mind to listen to a preacher and as soon as he says something that doesn't agree with their theology, they will start questioning everything he says from that point on. This should not be, because we have been told by God's Word to search the Scriptures out for ourselves.

So many Christians don't realize that their "gut feeling" is what their born-again spirit inside them is telling them. We need to take notice when something is not sitting right. Because these people don't really trust their spirit heart, they allow their mind in their soul to assert control over every decision that is made. I tend to think that the reason people say "love is blind" is because in matters of love, we often go with what our emotions are telling us, without consulting what God's Word says or what the Holy Spirit is saying to us. To our detriment, our human mind and emotions often cause our free will to make wrong decisions.

When the Holy Spirit comes into our life, He comes and takes up residence in our spirit/heart. We need to learn not to lean on our understanding/mind or feelings/emotions of our soul and we need to trust the Lord and follow our heart-spirit/Holy Spirit. Like anything of worth, trusting our spiritual heart in decisions rather than our gullible human mind, is a discipline that we need to both learn and overcome.

All of this may seem complicated but God has made it very simple for us - His Word tells us to: *"Trust in the Lord with all your heart, and lean not on your own understanding; in all your ways acknowledge Him, and He shall direct your paths."* *Proverbs 3:5-6*

In other words, we have to ignore what appears to be logical and do what our spirit is telling us to do. This can be hard at first, but it's the Christian way because it is the way God intended way back when He originally created Adam and Eve.

In summary: I therefore strongly encourage you to be that lonely or homeless person's new friend. Your friends might not join you and may even laugh at you. Your mind will scream at you, "What are you doing sitting here with this strange person? You're not going to achieve anything!" But ignore what your mind has to say and get to know that broken person and ask them how they came into such a situation. See if they are comfortable enough to share a meal with you. Yes, your flesh and your mind will scream and protest, but God will be happy.

Heavenly Father,

Teach us to listen to our born-again spirit more and more Father. In Jesus' name, I ask this. Amen.

Kingdom Nugget 65
Your Spirit is the Real You

Have you ever wanted to discover the real you? Our lives are so dominated by what our mind or emotions tell us that we can easily become confused. If we have experienced personal salvation, we will learn who we are by reading who God says we are, especially in the New Testament Epistles.

Man was created in the image of God. God is a spirit being. Therefore, we are foremost a spirit being. We have been given an eternal soul and we live in a temporary physical body. Our soul makes us different from anyone else. A healthy soul is very important to God, but it's not as important to Him as our spirit is. That's because, the real us is our eternal spirit/heart. As I have said: This isn't our physical heart, but it's our *gut feeling* in our spirit –deep down in our belly area. This is where our spirit is.

Jesus spoke to the woman at the well in John 4:13 and said: *"Whoever drinks of this water will thirst again, but whoever drinks of the water that I shall give him will never thirst. But the water that I shall give him will become in him a fountain of water springing up into everlasting life."*

Again, Jesus said in John 7:38 – *"He who believes in Me, as the Scripture has said, out of his heart will flow rivers of living water."* That's not our physical heart but our spirit/heart in our belly area.

The whole message of the Bible is to be accepted by God through faith in Him alone. God always honors our faith in Him and the atonement work of His Son, Jesus Christ. Every human being's spirit is precious to God and He wants to occupy it, as this was how it was before Adam and Eve sinned. When Satan won personal victory over them, future mankind lost that spiritual connection to their Creator. But Jesus, by defeating death, has changed the playing field big time for all of us who simply believe.

For the human spirit to be forever connected to God, it is absolutely necessary for every one of us to ask Jesus to come into our heart to be our Savior and Lord.

You have heard preachers say that it doesn't matter how many Scriptures you know in your head, what's important is that you know them in your heart of hearts. This means Scripture is only powerful when your spirit is engaging with God's truth. When your spirit does engage, it can be called a personal revelation from God. It takes much discipline to get a verse of Scripture from your mind deep down to your spirit. It may require constant meditation and repetition, but occasionally, it instantly clicks and when it does, you will have received a new revelation from God that you never had before.

Have you ever listened to a sermon and suddenly one sentence of the message really connected with you? That part of the message passed through your mind filter and actually impacted you in your spirit realm. When this happens, you should take that particular message away with you and repeat it to yourself until it becomes part of you.

For example: one simple cliché that has become part of my spirit goes like this: "There are no wrong questions. The only wrong question is the one I fail to ask."

As a teacher, I am eager to learn new things and so when someone is teaching and allows questions, I normally ask more than one. At first, I was embarrassed with doing this in public, but now, that cliché of mine has worked itself down into my spirit. Therefore, I do not hold back my questions.

Your spirit knows when you have not been told the correct interpretation to a certain Scripture. If you are like me, you might have hundreds of Scriptures that are silently waiting to be spoken about in a way that your heart accepts them. Your born-again spirit longs for truth and is pure, innocent and honest.

When we are born-again, we become like a child in our spirit. But our old thought patterns in our mind have soiled and corrupted our understanding. Don't continue to beat yourself up for what your mind spends its time thinking about. Our mind is part of our soul and the sanctification of our soul is a life-process, so just be assured that your mind is not the real you! God is doing His part in helping all Christians to renew their mind as they allow Him to do so.

Heavenly Father,

Reveal to us more and more of just how "You" see us Lord. In Jesus' name, I ask this. Amen.

Kingdom Nugget 66
Seeing Jesus for Who He is Now

When I privately pray for myself or for others, I don't usually end with the words "in Jesus name, I ask." God and Jesus know who I am and they know I am coming to them through the blood of Jesus. Still, you may strongly differ with me about my view, so you need to follow your own gut instinct. Actually, I only verbalize the name of Jesus, in these Kingdom Nuggets because it makes my readers more comfortable for a prayer to end that way. The sad things is, to many people that is all Jesus is – He is just a name that you finish a prayer with - to make sure that it receives Heaven's attention.

What I am saying is, that I often feel that Jesus is treated like an "accessory" that some people wear like a handbag or a piece of jewellery. Jesus may be part of who they are, but He isn't all that they are. Jesus wants us to be *consumed with Him* – HE IS the Lover of our soul!

Jesus has very deep emotions. I have seen Jesus cry when a friend of mine said that a demon was manifesting in me and was "pretending" to be Jesus. I saw a tear run down His cheek. I asked Him why he was crying and He said that some people have so much unbelief that nothing can be done to persuade them of the supernatural.

Jesus is very emotional and is not afraid to express His emotions to us, if we are open to Him.

Many so called modern prophets say that Jesus is angry with the world's system. Actually, God has good reason to be angry, the devil continually tells lies to the people Jesus died for! We need to understand that God in the Old Testament had to strongly discipline people because they had no inner spiritual understanding at that time. Jesus hadn't atoned for our sin and the Holy Spirit had not been poured out onto believers to give them spiritual understanding, way back then.

Yes, God was angry back in those days and He disciplined people quite harshly at times. However, all God's anger toward man was forever heaped onto Jesus as He hung on the Cross. *God is therefore not angry at anyone anymore!* God loves the whole world and longs for everyone to welcome Him as Savior and eventually as Lord of their life. Sin has been appeased once and for all.

Any loving parent understands that until a young child can reason for themselves in a wise manner, he or she needs to have some form of discipline to teach them right from wrong so that they comply with necessary instructions. Otherwise, they can harm themselves or others.

Nevertheless, I have to tell you that Jesus weeps for the state of the world and all the injustice and suffering in it. Jesus loves all mankind – to Him, no one is un-redeemable! Both Jesus and His Father weep for the many thousands of people who die each day from preventable causes. Jesus also weeps for all the people in slavery around the world. Jesus weeps for that lady in your church whose husband stays at home drinking on a Sunday, watching sports. Jesus weeps for all the girls and boys who are being molested by family members.

Many people have in their mind, a mystical Jesus in Heaven full of joy and happiness! These people think that Heaven is a place full of joy where there is no sorrow and that is true. But Heaven is not a place where uncomfortable subjects like slavery on earth, child sexual abuse and poverty are swept under the carpet and not talked about. Heaven is a place where Jesus and His Father can see all that is happening on earth and they weep and pray for its inhabitants.

It's too easy to think that Jesus has all the answers! He does, but man exercises his free will many times opposite to the will of God! There is therefore sadness in Heaven! Sin saddens God. Because we are doing enough for people who are caught in the sex trade, or for people trapped in poverty, or for people who have not heard the Gospel, we tend to put some of those bad subjects out of our mind. We may even praise God each week at church without ever a thought for such people. Jesus is always aware of those less fortunate and I believe that He cries for our indifference and for all those who are abused in any way.

There is a room in Heaven that Jesus goes to. This room is called the Crying Room. In this room, He can see all the suffering in the world and He weeps and intercedes for all the broken ones. I cry for Jesus. My heart is heavy as a write this. You see, Jesus needs friends that will weep with Him and help Him carry His burden.

Jesus needs people who don't come to Him in prayer with a shopping list of demands, but simply to come and weep with Him about all the injustices of the world. So what can we do for Jesus? He longs for a family of people who will do anything and give anything to stop the suffering in this world. Jesus would love His people who are called by His name to lay down their idols and anything else that consumes them with the love of the things of this world, and to follow Him into the darkness in order to bring His light to dispel the devil's darkness.

Some people wonder where I get such sensitivity to Jesus. They wonder how I receive these secrets from God. It is because I have spent thousands of hours speaking with Jesus and I am His friend. I am a slave to Jesus and will do and write anything He tells me to do or say.

Heavenly Father,

Draw every one of my readers closer to your Son, Jesus. Take their fear away and let them embrace Jesus for who He really is. In Jesus' name, I ask this. Amen.

Kingdom Nugget 67
Asking Jesus Questions

When you go out to a cafe with a new friend, much of your conversation is made up of simple basic questions. When the person replies, you listen and then many times, you ask another question based on what they said. Over time, each of you will be communicating with each other on a new level and the intimacy of the friendship deepens.

When people ask me how they can grow closer to Jesus, I tell them to ask Him questions like we do with friends on earth. Jesus has multitudes of answers waiting for you. He is aware of the questions that you are going to ask, and I believe His Holy Spirit is actually prompting you to ask these questions.

You can ask Jesus anything. He is far more willing to grow closer to you and to share His heart with, than you are with Him. As an example: You could ask Him what He thinks of your country and its leaders; your country's foreign policy; your church; your pastor; or anything that concerns you. You can ask Him all manner of questions. The more you ask Him, the deeper your relationship with Him will become. You will find that Jesus is interested in the smallest things in your life as well as the big things. In this way, you will discover that He is not just interested in you serving Him. No, He wants far more than that as He wants to have a deep personal and even an intimate relationship with you.

Many people wonder about the different Bible characters or they have questions about certain decisions that these people made. However, we don't have to wonder any more about these things. When you start to speak to Jesus, you can ask Him about all the things you really want to know about.

Every part of the Bible becomes more exciting as you ask Jesus questions about the things you read. All in all, your life becomes a whole lot more interesting when you ask Jesus questions. Soon, you will be carried away just communing with Jesus and the hours will slip away. Prayer will certainly not be a laborious thing to you, because it will be a day-long event as you conduct your everyday life.

Heavenly Father,

Give the readers the inspiration to ask Jesus questions from this day on. I ask this in Jesus' name. Amen.

Walking With the Holy Spirit

The Christian life should not be boring and eventless. It should have destiny, desire and purpose. It's hard to walk with purpose if we are not aware of our destiny. Therefore, we all need to seek God about these things. Then, when we discover what we were created to do, we can then follow the leading of the Holy Spirit and walk in that calling.

The Holy Spirit wants to be your friend. He wants to be your guide and to show you things and lead you on His path. Many Christians experience the presence of the Holy Spirit during worship time at church and they can even testify that the Holy Spirit illuminates the Scriptures to them, by revealing things that had gone unnoticed before. However, sadly, very few Christians can honestly say that the Holy Spirit is a really close personal friend of theirs.

Personal Testimony: There are times when I am led by the Holy Spirit into a divine encounter without my knowledge. Today, that happened to me as I met for the third time a new friend from a church I have been attending. This is a very spiritual girl and the last time I was with her, she asked me to pray that she might be able to go to Heaven in a vision.

Today, while I was out, I felt led to go and check out what movies were on. Because there wasn't any I wanted to see, I went outside to wait for the bus. Walking past the bus stop was this same young girl and she waved to me and said Hello. She said that Jesus told her to come to this suburb, more than forty minutes from her place, and so I suggested to her that I should take her on a vision to Heaven today. We went upstairs and sat down in the shopping center and within just a few minutes, she was happily interacting with a young girl in Heaven.

Sleeping in today may not have been the Holy Spirit's plan, but certainly going to check out the movies was a work of the Holy Spirit. The young lady followed the voice of Jesus today which was given to her through the vehicle of the Holy Spirit. And the Holy Spirit certainly assisted me, as I took her on a trip to Heaven like He has shown me to do with other people.

I walk quite a distance to the railway station and I used to get wet when it rained until I asked the Holy Spirit to prompt me when to take an umbrella and He has done that for me ever since. He will also tell me other things to take out with me – perhaps a certain book or my Bible. If He tells me to take my Bible on the train, I know that I am going to need it that day.

People think it's really great to be friendly with Jesus and to be a friend of God's and yet, very often, they will shy away from any talk of friendship with the Holy Spirit. I can understand their concern, but no one is going to do anything really great in the Kingdom of God, without having personal sensitivity to the Holy Spirit.

He is wonderful and such a better writer than me. Every time I sit down to write, I need to feel His anointing on me, or else my words do not flow easy. I would rather admit that the Holy Spirit is my co-writer and give God glory, than sit down without His presence on me.

The way that I am led by the Holy Spirit is to be constantly aware of His leading. Rather than just thinking to myself that I'll go to the shops and check out the movies, Jesus or the Holy Spirit could say, "Go down to that shopping center, there is someone I want you to meet." I find it a lot more exciting to be consciously led by Jesus and the Holy Spirit, than it is to be simply led by my own personal thoughts.

God knows that I really want to be led by the Holy Spirit and His Son and because I have shown a willingness to obey His promptings when it comes to doing Kingdom work, I am sure that He has allowed the leadings to increase. God knows I am always open to bring a prophetic word, so He leads me to give many of them to total strangers or anyone else I meet.

Dear Jesus,

Place a desire in the reader's heart to be continually led by Your Holy Spirit. Encourage the reader to draw closer to Your Holy Spirit.

Kingdom Nugget 69
Sharing Your Life
With Jesus

I consider it to be such a joy to be inspired to write and to be able to write two or three posts or nuggets in this book within one sitting, yet what happens to me when depression sets in? At these times, it is easy to withdraw from everyone, even from Jesus. Yet, when things get really tough, I find that I just have to share my pain with Him.

It's wonderful to have a loving Savior in Heaven who knows your whole life and who accepts you with all your faults and has answers to your questions. Even in the midst of being down, Jesus has words that ignite my spirit and make me come alive.

I want you to know that Jesus really has a vested interest in talking to you and being involved in your life. Sometimes, we don't think that we can bring Him any glory, but just getting up from a sad pit and giving Him praise for it, gives Him much glory go on with it can be a living testimony to others who are, or have been through a hard time. Of course, Jesus is there in the good times. He loves to laugh with us when we are laughing, He loves to cheer us on when we are stretching and striving to meet a goal, and He loves to share His love with us with the wonderful little things He has to say to us. He is a great man to have in your life, a man that no man on earth can possibly equal. For all that are single like me, He is a comfort and a real friend in time of need. Talk to Him and even if you cannot hear Him speak back to yet, share your heart of hearts with Him. Hold nothing back. If you are frustrated with Him and life, let Him know. He has broad shoulders and He loves us when we are really honest with Him. Sharing my life with Jesus these last couple of years has been very rewarding for me. Simply sitting down to write these nuggets and feeling His Spirit on me has been a joy. The closer you get to Jesus, the more you discuss with Him, the more you are used by Him, the more fulfilling life can get. Jesus is an awesome friend to me. Many thousands of nights I have laid in bed talking to Him before I go to sleep. Many days He has been with me all day. He is my Master and my Friend.

Have you invested much of your heart with Jesus? Every friendship gets richer the more that you share and put out there. Take a risk with Jesus and purpose to get really serious with Him and open right up to Him. You won't regret it.

Father

Give people the courage to draw close to Your and live their lives out in the open bare before Jesus in word and deed. In Jesus name I ask. Amen. Always, know that Jesus knows what it is like to be sad, or to be lonely, and even to be misunderstood. He never had an easy life and He has not promised us an easy life either. Jesus was physically crucified and in a much less painful way, He wants us to be like His servant Paul who said:

"I have been crucified with Christ; it is no longer I who live, but Christ lives in me; and the life which I now live in the flesh, I live by faith in the Son of God, who loved me and gave Himself for me." Galatians 2:20

A few chapters later, Paul said *"Let us not grow weary while doing good, for in due season, we shall reap if we do not lose heart. Therefore, as we have opportunity, let us do good to all, especially to those who are of the household of faith." Galatians 6:9-10*

Prayer – Why Do You Pray?

You can go to any large Christian bookshop or type in the word "prayer" in Amazon books online and there seems to be a mountain of such books instructing us on how we are to pray. However, I tend to think that many people just read these books for head knowledge, rather than to take the time to actually pray as the author suggests. No amount of knowledge on prayer will replace the personal daily practice of setting time apart specifically to talk to God.

The only book I have totally read on prayer is called "A Better way to pray," by Andrew Wommack. This book may probably first upset you before it will make you happy! Why? I say this because the information that Andrew shares in this book blows out of the water many modern concepts and ideas about effective praying.

I believe that Andrew is a fantastic author and his book on prayer is a really great book. I think it is under ten dollars on Kindle and I highly recommend it, but I know so many people have an aversion to spending money on resources, so I am going to write some Nuggets about some of the key points that the book raises.

Why do believers pray? Does prayer erase our conscience? Do we pray in order to rid ourselves of feeling dirty because of the sins in our life? Do we take our dirty washing to God and ask him to wash us and make us all brand new again? Can you imagine how God feels about that type of thinking? I am not saying that we don't have to be forgiven, but we don't have to bring a whole list of wrongdoings and confess them all in detail. *God knows what we did*. We can simply ask for His grace to help us not to do it again.

Do you come to God with your shopping list of desires and wants? Is that why you pray? First you confess your sins and get washed in the blood, and then it's time to ask for things? I suspect that getting clean and getting "things" may be the two major reasons many Christians pray to God. If it is, realize that these two reasons for prayer are actually just all about you.

What about coming to The Father through Jesus His Son and to simply acknowledge the awesomeness of being in their presence and then have a conversation with God for a while. What about resting in His presence and spending quality time with Him just loving on Him and thanking Him for being such an important part of your life?

Here is a Facebook post from one of my dear friends that has a very close relationship with Jesus. Do your prayers resemble the following?

"Twenty-four hours ago, Jesus was the first One to acknowledge me on my birthday. A little after midnight... we were in my prayer closet talking and He was holding my left hand... then He said, 'I love you'... tears started to roll down my face. 'Feel My heart.' I stretched my right hand to His heart and could feel it beating. 'It comes alive when you spend time with Me... it beats for you.'

When I am with Him, everything else just fades away. Yes, it was definitely the best birthday ever."

Don't you think it is time to love Father God and Jesus and simply hang out with Them like this friend of mine?

Kingdom Nugget 71
Praying Because...
We Must

I have battled for twenty years with the spirit of antichrist who masquerades as the voice of Jesus to me. This evil spirit tricks me into believing that it is the Lord Jesus who is speaking to me. At one time, I become so sick and tired of being fooled, by not being able to correctly identify the voice I heard, that I told Jesus to stop speaking to me and I stopped speaking to Him. To my amazement, I didn't lose my faith in that year, yet in all that time, I didn't speak to Jesus or the false Jesus and neither did they speak to me.

One day in the rain, I could not find my key to fit the caravan I was sleeping in. I had searched through my whole key ring twice, trying every key. In the meantime, I was getting soaked! In desperation, I asked Jesus which key it was. He told me it was the third on the right. I turned to it and put it in the key hole and opened the caravan.

Why did I share that story with you? My faith did not suffer in that year! Neither was I lied to by the false Jesus so I wasn't tripped up by a demon. Do you know the really good thing that happened? That year, I actually learned to stand more on what the Word of God was saying to me. Praise the Lord! The devil must have hated that. The word of God is sure and perfect, *it will accomplish the purpose that God has for it!* Voices can be very deceptive.

Don't ever make the mistake that many people make, by coming to God as a form of religion. God hates all forms of religion. Christianity is a relationship, not a religion. A religion is man trying to reach up to God but Christianity is God lovingly reaching down to mankind.

As Christians, we are told that we have to pray and if we are not praying for half an hour per day, we are simply not growing in faith. The way I see it, so many of us simply don't have enough spiritual things going on in our life, and because we don't know how to pray, we languish after ten minutes. Then we feel guilty because we didn't spend a half hour in prayer.

Let's put this whole scenario in a different light. If you were happily married, and you were having dinner at night, do you think that you would run out of things to say to your loved one after ten minutes? And how would it be if you spent five of those ten minutes saying everything you did wrong that day and the remaining five minutes you spent begging your spouse to do things for you? That type of ten minute conversation wouldn't last very long. I'm sure your spouse would suggest a better way to converse at the evening meal time.

God doesn't need you to laboriously spend half an hour with him. He is delighted if you only give him a joyful five minutes chat in the morning and five minutes in the night time. He doesn't mind if your prayer time is while you are in the shower or in the car going to work or whatever. He loves you and He simply would love to spend any time with you.

God wants us to enjoy spending time with Him. No loved one would want you to spend time with them when underneath you resent them for requiring it of you. God adores you and wants your time with Him to be special. He doesn't want this special time with Him to be done out of duty or in order to keep up appearances.

All great relationships need to be transparent. There are to be no hidden objectives or obligations put on either party. God absolutely delights in us just seeking His friendship and talking to Him as we would our very closest friend. Time should never be an issue. A good marriage results when two very different characters take time to appreciate their mate for who he is. God simply wants the same in our prayer life.

Dear Jesus,

Open the eyes of your bride as You woo her, dear Jesus so that she in turn will woo You.

Talking to Your Best Friend

The world will entice us away from our Lover. When you have forsaken the lusts and pleasures of this world and when you know Jesus as a very close friend, prayer becomes a delight. When Jesus is your very closest friend, then spending time with Him is not a chore but it's like a nice steak dinner, something to be savored and enjoyed.

I know it is possible to have an intimate walk with Jesus, because I do. I also know I could go far deeper with Him because I personally know people who have a deeper walk with Him than I do. So don't look at my posts and my life and say to yourself, "that's okay for Matthew to say, but I couldn't ever be as close to Jesus as he is!" No, don't ever think that way.

Twenty-five years ago, I had a rich friend who was very successful. In fact he was a millionaire. He shared the following words at a conference that I attended.

"Every step to the top is a normal step. It is just one foot in front of the other. Every time I show this business of mine to another prospect, I simply am taking the risk of being rejected or laughed at. But when you go on a trip and take the last step, on to the top of a mountain where I am, the view is very different." He had achieved a level in the Amway business that only one in a million or so distributors ever reach.

I will never forget his statement. The first step to becoming closer and more intimate with Jesus is the same size steps that I take now. It is just that my view is different to yours. Take that first step and become a deep and abiding friend of Jesus and your prayer life will reach new levels. You will see things from God's perspective and you will be excited to be part of His overall plan for the world. You will also be made aware of just how much He loves you and is delighted to have your friendship.

Dear Jesus,

Show my reader what it is to be a friend of Yours. Show them what it takes to be in this world but not "of" this world. Lead them step by step, to a place where they can re-read all these Nuggets again. Let each nugget become simple to them and eventually become common knowledge to them so they can pass them on to others. Amen.

Kingdom Nugget 73
Don't Ever Try to Twist God's Arm

There all sorts of strange ideas about prayer.

For example: You are earnestly praying for a husband of God's choice. God has heard your prayers and is actually working on a particular gentleman right now and he should be ready for marriage in five years time. God plans on refining this man's character by humbling him for a short time in order to become a real friend of God. Would you be able to trust God to provide a great husband even if it was to take five years? Or would you prefer to be married sooner to a man who had a weaker character, rather than wait for God's best for you?

You can beg God, you even can storm Heaven every night for three years and yet if you are not getting your way and you still are not due to meet your spouse for another year, do you think your prayers are really getting you what you need or desire?

What if, in the third year, you wanted to twist God's arm and apply some pressure on Him? What if you went on a two week fast for your future husband to manifest? Do you think seeing that you are still a year off, that God is going to bring your husband to you a year early because of your two week fast?

I bring this illustration to you not to mock you, but to demonstrate that some people have misguided conceptions about prayer and fasting. These people believe that if they harass God enough and storm Heaven with their requests, then God will give them their desire. They will disregard God's perfect wisdom and timing for the sake of getting their prayer answered how and when they want. This type of believer really thinks that by prayer accompanied by fasting, that they can literally twist God's arm, so to speak.

There are many books written on fasting which I have not read, but my general opinion is that many people approach fasting as a bribe to getting their own way. If God tells you to fast then by all means do so – I am not saying that fasting is not spiritually beneficial. One good thing about fasting is that is reduces your lust of the flesh and because your fleshy desires are being denied, then your spirit can become very strong! Therefore, the effectual prayer of a righteous man (or woman) can avail much, just as the Apostle James has told us.

Many times, we are praying for things that God doesn't want to give us, or does not want to give us just yet! For example: At fourteen years of age, I felt the call on my life to preach. At thirty, I still had not preached! Then one day, Jesus told me that I could not enter a Bible college and become a pastor the normal way but He was going to teach me Himself.

About nine years ago, I learned that I was to become a prophet. Since then, I have spent quite a bit of time working out how to be a prophet. To date, I have only preached three times in my life. But for thirty-two years, I have waited for God to give me a wide-open door to regularly preach.

God however, has been very good to me in the following way: Six thousand people per month read one of my teaching articles. Three thousand people per month watch one of my videos. Two years ago, I wrote a book called, "The Parables of Jesus Made Simple" and to date, six thousand, five hundred people have downloaded it.

The point I am making is that I'm still not physically preaching in a pulpit each week. How do you think my continual prayer for an open door to preach, would have influenced God over all these years? Do you think He would open one because I pleaded or is He still doing a precious work in me to make me a great preacher when He starts to open doors?

What about romance for me? I have been single for twenty-one years now. How far away is my next wife? Are we ever going to meet? Six prophets have told me that she is coming for me. Do I make her come faster by prayer or do I simply wait on God for His timing and pray instead for her spirit to be renewed and refreshed each day until she meets me?

What good would I do storming Heaven, when my future wife may be another five or ten years away? I am not going to try to twist God's arm in any way. It is futile. I need to remain patient and ready for God's perfect timing. I have been instructed in God's Word to: *"Trust in the Lord, and do good; dwell in the land, and feed on His faithfulness. Delight yourself also in the Lord, and He shall give you the desires of your heart. Commit your way to the Lord, trust also in Him, and He shall bring it to pass." Psalm 37:3-5.* How plain is that!

Heavenly Father,

Let this message in this Nugget speak to my readers in such a way that they have never seen before. Teach them to rely on Your leading for prayer and not for what they think they want or desire. In Jesus' name, I ask. Amen.

Kingdom Nugget 74
How Much is Enough Prayer?

Let's say that you have prayed for ten minutes in the morning and again for ten minutes in the evening and yet, you still have this question, "Am I praying enough?"

While that is a fair question, I want you to realize that if *we put any limits on prayer, the whole thing becomes religious!* Religion in any form brings to us, guilt and condemnation from the enemy. He forever wants to attack us and pull us down in any way he can. A far better question would be: "Am I happy with the time I spend with the Lord?"

If you are happy, then that is a good thing. It's just like any other relationship. If you have a partner and only have twenty minutes of personal time with them each day, away from distractions and away from the children, you really treasure that time with them. Your relationship could be really healthy and strong with that amount of time. Similarly, your relationship with Jesus could be really strong with only five minutes face to face time each day. Some people really love to pray, so for them, half an hour is not a long time to pray. This does not make them better than you or I, it's just the way that they are.

Prayer is connecting with God. Prayer is something that we should enjoy, and it should not be something that we are made to feel guilty about if we don't think we are doing enough.

In Kingdom Nugget (71), I spoke about how I didn't speak to Jesus for a whole year. I told how my relationship with God grew in that year by reading the Word of God. I am by no means suggesting that others should imitate me, but what I am saying is that you should not feel guilty if all you are managing each day is five minutes with the Lord. Guilt comes from the devil himself, so don't allow him to ever rob you of the joy of the Lord.

Satan can use other Christians, books and pastors to make you feel like less of a person if you are not reading your Word each day and spending a good amount of time in prayer. Believe me: God is already happy with you. You will not impress Him with how much time you spend in prayer. God is after "quality" face to face time, He is not after "quantity" time.

God can never love you less than He has always loved you. In the same way, God will never love you more than He has ever loved you. I say this because His love for any of us is not related in any way to your performance level. As a believer, His love for you is based purely on who you are in Christ. His Holy Spirit residing in your human spirit causes God to always see you in Christ, even when you feel that you have let God down in some way. Don't ever let the devil or other people minimize God's love for you.

Heavenly Father,

I ask that You will use these nuggets to strip away any guilt from Your people in the subject of prayer. In Jesus' name, I ask. Amen.

The Prayer That Never Ceases

I never knew what the prayer that never ceases was all about until Andrew Wommack in his book, "A Better way to Pray" shared with me what it was. I am very thankful as this is something that I do, most days.

The Lord was talking to this anointed Pastor and teacher about prayer and He used an illustration to get Andrew's attention. God said to him, "Andrew, would you like to spend one hour with your wife today all alone with her to talk over dinner, or would you prefer to spend the whole day with her as she shops and goes about her business?" Andrew said he would prefer to spend the whole day with his wife. God then said, "so why do you limit your time with me, to just an hour a day when you can fellowship with me all day long?"

Andrew had never heard it like that before. I guess if you are anything like me, you might not have heard it like that before either. If you can have God go with you all day and hang out with Him while you are doing your business each day, wouldn't you choose that over just one hour a day in prayer?

Spending all day in the presence of God, talking to Him about whatever, is what people refer to as the prayer without ceasing. This is not being in prayer in your prayer closet all day, every day. It is being God conscious all day every day! You are automatically involving Him in all the moment by moment decisions in your everyday life.

When I read that in Andrew's book I realized that without knowing it, I had been participating in praying without ceasing. No longer will I feel guilty for not praying enough, or praying like other people. No longer, will I be bound up by religion that dictates that we must pray all the time. My life is one continual prayer, as I walk each day in the power of the Holy Spirit and I am very aware of God walking along side of me all the time.

That's probably why I love to do prophetic evangelism on the streets of Sydney, because there are so many people who God really wants to talk to as I go about my business.

Heavenly Father,

Teach the reader to have You on their mind each day and to take You everywhere with them and involve You in every decision. In Jesus' name, I ask. Amen.

Kingdom Nugget 76
Using Mustard Seed Faith

I suspect that erroneous beliefs concerning prayer cause the most heartache in the lives of many believers. It is a subject that is close to God's heart because it is all about enriching a personal relationship with Him. However, the whole subject of prayer is very often misunderstood and can even become downgraded to a religious activity. Like I have said - book stores are full of information about it, yet people still don't seem to be able to pray and get the results that they want and need.

A mustard seed is the smallest seed of any tree, so what is this prayer that is so small in faith, but has the capacity to move a mountain that Jesus spoke about in Mark's Gospel?

Let me try to explain: Have you ever seen a child who is coming last in a race as he crosses the finish line? When children are young, they are not cut up and sad if they don't win. Little children just run the race right to the end: they are full of smiles that they actually finished and they are caught up in the joy that they were even considered to be part of the race.

Every believer needs to be like that child! We simply have to have the courage to enter the race of faith. We may not be the most eloquent of prayer warriors or we might not be the head intercessor at church. We may not even have been a Christian for very long. However, we simply have been given the privilege to enter the race of faith and offer up a prayer to God just as His little child competes in any physical race.

A mountain can be anything: it can be any obstacle in your life. In my case, my mountain was my own father who had a very bad anger issue all his life and to me, I seemed to cop the brunt of it. In childlike faith, I asked God to make an intervention in my father's life so he would cease being angry all the time.

I recently spent two weeks with my parents in Coffs Harbour and it came home to me in a fresh new way how much my father has changed. He is not the fiery man he used to be and he said not to leave it too long before I return. He loved having me around. God is so good.

I remember that one time in the past, I had been talking to Jesus and He asked me if I would agree for Him to send my father to Hell if he allowed me to be the human vessel in the salvation of ten thousand people who otherwise would remain unsaved.

I was speechless in shock wondering how Jesus could send my Christian father to Hell. I asked Jesus: "Is this real?" He said it was.

I asked, how long can I think about it? He said: "Think about it for as long as you like."

Three days later I told him with tears running down my cheeks: "If this really is the way it has to be, and ten thousand people will be saved if my father is sent to Hell, than I would be the most selfish person in the world to keep my father."

I was totally distraught, I could hardly speak, but I said "Let it be, Jesus. I want you to save those ten thousand people even if my own father goes to Hell."

Jesus said to me, "I am not going to send your father to Hell, Matthew! But do you know how you suffered over the last three days about your father going to Hell?"

I said, "Yes! It was so horrible!"

Jesus said, "Well, that is how you should feel about anyone you meet, who is going to Hell!"

That was an awesome insight to me and I know that I have become a much more effective prophetic evangelist since that day. I think that experience about my father and all my emotion that I carried about my angry dad, actually caused Jesus to bring an apostle into my father's life to rebuke him and show him how to change into a happy man. That actually happened in 2005.

We don't have to have much faith to be effective, just be like a little child in the race of faith!

Dear Jesus,

Teach us all to be children as we pray with the innocent faith of a child with no worries.

Kingdom Nugget 77
Tongues

I am not sure I could do a subject on prayer and not mention the gift of tongues. For many people reading this, who are not baptized in the Holy Spirit, this post might be a waste of time, but even if that includes you, I'd like you to take the time to read my testimony.

From a young boy, my spiritual home was the local Baptist church in Coffs Harbour, New South Wales. I later moved to Queensland. I had been converted at the age of eight but I had never been water baptized as a believer and I knew that Jesus wanted me to do this. I was twenty seven at the time and was going to a Pentecostal church. This was not long after my wife of two years had left me for another man. However, nothing was further from my mind on that momentous occasion of my baptism, that Jesus would choose to also baptize me in the Holy Spirit.

I never realized this at the time, but about a week after my water baptism, I was praying for my wife. In hindsight, it was definitely a selfish prayer I was praying. I was praying that God's best would happen to her and that she would break up with her new boyfriend and come back to me.

I became frustrated with my prayer. I felt my own emotions were getting in the way of God's will and then, out of the blue, I just started hearing myself praying a prayer that didn't originate in my own mind. I could hear myself praying a prayer in English that was the most perfect prayer that could ever be prayed for my wife. Before the prayer that was effortlessly rolling off my tongue was finished, my cheeks were running with tears.

After I finished praying I asked Jesus, "What was that?"

He said: *"That is the gift of tongues, Matthew and it is yours for the taking when you are comfortable about it."*

Since that time, I don't often pray in tongues as I feel that I only have about one sentence in my Heavenly prayer language. Because it has never really developed, I thought that there was no use trying, but I feel that God has taught me to pray Holy Spirit led prayers in English like that prayer that came from my mouth for my former wife that day.

For those who regularly pray in tongues, it is the best way to pray because the Holy Spirit prays on your behalf and we all know if the Holy Spirit Himself prayed a prayer, it would certainly be answered.

Heavenly Father,

Give people the courage to seek this gift in their lives. In Jesus' name, I ask. Amen.

Closing thoughts

It is my hope that you have enjoyed this book. I have read this book when it was Kingdom Nuggets three times, and listened to it as an audio book four times. If you go to Audible you can find this book under my name as Kingdom Nuggets. Or you can follow this link on Kindle:

http://tinyurl.com/oqo7u9d

It is one thing to listen to a sermon, or to read a book, it is quite another to apply that book or sermon. I have shared how to find intimacy with Jesus and made it sound simple in this book, but in order for that to happen to you, you need to meditate on these truths. I suggest you buy the audio book and listen to it as you surf the internet and post on Facebook. You can even download the audio app to your smart phone and listen to the book as you go to work each day.

I have a very deep and close relationship with Jesus and much of this book was written by my knowledge, and yet much of the information about Jesus was revelation right out of Heaven via the Holy Spirit. It is this revelation that I listen to over and over again so that I can get it down into my spirit.

It is my prayer that each of you might grow each day and each year to the point that I find my relationship with Jesus and even surpass me.

I'd love to hear from you

One really easy way to bless me is to write a short and honest review of this book on Amazon. It costs you nothing and it is a really wonderful way of letting other people know that this was an encouraging book to read. Before I buy any book personally, I make sure that I read the reviews on Amazon and if I am convinced by them, I make my purchase. I won't even download a free book, unless it has good reviews.

I personally read all the reviews that my books get and you can be sure that I will read your review.

Please feel free to also share a link to my book on Facebook with your friends, sharing in a short note with them why they would enjoy it.

To contact me:

You can write to my email address at survivors.sanctuary@gmail.com.

You can donate money to my book writing ministry, or request a personal prophecy at http://personal-prophecy-today.com.

How to Sponsor a Book Project

If you have been blessed by this book, you might consider sponsoring a book for me. It normally costs me between fifteen hundred and two thousand dollars or more to produce each book that I write, depending on the length of the book.

If you seek the Holy Spirit about financing a book for me, I know that the Lord would be eternally grateful to you. Consider how much this book has blessed you and then think of hundreds or even thousands of people who would be blessed by a book of mine. As you are probably aware, the vast majority of my books are ninety-nine cents on Kindle, which proves to you that book writing is indeed a ministry for me and not a money- making venture. I would be very happy if you supported me in this.

If you have any questions for me or if you want to know what projects I am currently working on that your money might finance, you can write to me at survivors.sanctuary@gmail.com and ask me for more information. I would be pleased to give you more details about my projects. You can sow any amount to my ministry by simply sending me money via the PayPal link at this address: http://personal-prophecy-today.com/support-my-ministry/ You can be sure that your support, no matter the amount, will be used for the publishing of helpful Christian books for people to read.

Other Books
by Matthew Robert Payne

If you enjoyed this book, you may enjoy other books by Matthew Robert Payne.

The Parables of Jesus Made Simple

The Prophetic Supernatural Experience

Prophetic Evangelism Made Simple

His Redeeming Love – A Memoir

Writing and Self Publishing Christian Nonfiction

Your Identity in Christ

Coping with your Pain and Suffering

Living for Eternity

Great Cloud of Witnesses Speak

Jesus Speaks Today

My Radical Encounters with Angels

You can find these books on Amazon at this link
http://tinyurl.com/pcqb66f

About the Author

Matthew was born again at the age of eight in a Baptist Church and quickly developed the ability to speak to Jesus, and have Jesus speak back to him. With a life that has seen much sorrow, he has developed a keen sense of compassion for all sorts of people.

Called as a prophet from birth, it wasn't till 2005 that he realized that he was called as a prophet. Over the past twenty years, he has been used by God to deliver over twenty thousand personal prophecies to people, the majority of which were given to total strangers. Matthew is well versed in hearing Jesus speak through him

With an intimate relationship with Jesus, Matthew lives to lead people closer to the Jesus that he has come to know so well. Matthew does much of his teaching today on YouTube and through books on Amazon. Through this book, Matthew hopes people may come to trust Jesus more and walk closer with Him as they apply these lessons. It is Matthew's prayer that you might find this book on Audible or Kingdom Nuggets that was produced before this publication was printed, and listen to it many times to get it down into your spirit.